BIRDS of PREY

HUNTERS OF THE SKY

by ALAN RICHARDS

COURAGE BOOKS

AN IMPRINT OF RUNNING PRESS
PHILADELPHIA · LONDON

9 8 7 6 5 4 3 2 1

Digit on the right indicates the number of this printing

This book was designed and produced by
Todtri Productions Limited
P.O. Box 572
New York, NY 10116-0572
FAX: (212) 279-1241

Printed and bound in Singapore

ISBN 0-7624-0286-5
Library of Congress Cataloging-in-Publication Number 93-159547

Publisher: Robert M. Tod
Designer and Art Director: Mark Weinberg
Editor: Mary Forsell
Typeset and Page Makeup: Strong Silent Type/NYC
Cover design: Betty Barnstable

Published by
Courage Books, an imprint of
Running Press Book Publishers
125 South Twenty-second Street
Philadelphia, Pennsylvania 19103-4399

TABLE OF CONTENTS

INTRODUCTION

Any bird that takes another living creature as part of its normal food intake can be claimed as a bird of prey. The term should therefore equally apply to a Kingfisher that seizes a fish as it plunge dives into the water, or to a Heron that stalks and spears a frog in the shallows, or even to a Thrush that pulls up a worm from the back garden lawn—they are all taking prey!

However the expression "bird of prey" is more usually applied to those birds belonging to the higher specialized order of birds, namely the Falconiformes: the hawks, eagles, falcons, and others—in fact it is this order of birds alone that some purists will accept as the only true birds of prey.

For the purposes of this book we extend our coverage to include the owls (Strigiformes), whose hunting behavior is very similar to their diurnal (daytime) counterparts—whereas the majority of owls are nocturnal and hunt at night.

There are two orders that comprise the birds profiled in this volume, the Falconiformes and the Strigiformes. They are subdivided as follows:

Falconiformes comprise four distinct families, namely:
1. The New World vultures (Cathartidae)
2. Osprey, hawks, and kites, etc. (Accipitridae)
3. The secretary birds (Sagittaridae)
4. Caracaras and falcons (Falconidae)

The Owls belong to the order Strigiformes and comprise two families, namely:
1. The bay or barn owls (Tytonidae)
2. The wood owls (Strigidae)

A more definitive term used to describe the Falconiformes is "raptor." This word is derived from the Latin *raptare*, meaning "to seize and carry off," which is exactly what many birds of prey do with their food.

Following are discussions of each major family listed above, with the exception of Sagittaridae, the Secretary Birds, as there is only one bird in this category.

Birds of prey are broadly distinguished by their hooked beaks, which are sharp and pointed and capable of tearing the flesh of their prey. Generally the feet are powerful, with strong talons used for gripping and killing their prey. However, in the case of the vultures the feet are quite small and generally play little part in the feeding action.

Within each major category of this book, I have profiled as many significant species as space here allows. It would take several volumes to fully discuss and depict each bird species. Therefore, I have also included photographs, accompanied by identifying captions, of additional species that share similar characteristics with those that are featured within each category. This is both to enrich the reader's understanding and increase visual awareness of birds not discussed in the main body of text.

OUTLINE OF THE VULTURES: CATHARTIDAE AND ACCIPITRIDAE

American Vultures, which belong to the family Cathartidae, may well have been much more widespread throughout the world than they are today, as fossils of their ancestors have been found in Europe as well as their current home ground. Some fossils discovered in California include the remains of species larger than any living today. One of them, named *Tetratornis incredibilis*, had a wing span of seventeen feet; others had wing spans of twelve to fourteen feet.

Today there are seven species of New World Vultures, or Condors, all of which are to be found in the Americas. Two of them are the largest living flying birds in current existence. One of them, the California Condor (see text entry), however, is on the verge of extinction. The other one, the Andean condor, as the name suggests, is found along the Andean range and occurs from Venezuela and Columbia southward to the Strait of Magellan. Though a relatively rare bird, the Andean Condor is not on the verge of extinction like its North American cousin. Living in a relatively sparsely populated region, its chances of being persecuted are greatly lessened. Both the California and Andean condors have wing spans of about ten feet and can weigh twenty to twenty-five pounds.

The third largest of the New World Vultures is the King Vulture, a handsome bird with the naked head brilliantly colored in a variety of green and purple hues. The bill is reddish orange with a black base, large red carnacle, and cere. The plumage is mostly black and white. As others of its family, it is a scavenger, but haunting rain forest and savannah. Unlike other New World Vultures it does not scavenge refuse round human dwellings.

Perhaps the most well known of the New World Vultures are the Black Vulture and the Turkey Vulture, both widely distributed from the northern United States to the South. A common sight as they soar overhead on motionless wings, they are often wrongly called "buzzards," which are different group of birds altogether.

As with all vultures, these two species have equally unsavory feeding habits and will eat anything they can locate, which with their keen sight appears to be no problem, while there is speculation that smell also plays a major role in their search for food.

There is also another species in this family, the Yellow-headed Vulture, which is found in Mexico southward to Argentina and Uruguay.

Though New World Vultures have hooked beaks for tearing flesh, their feet are not designed to play any part in feeding. Their toes are long and slender with only slight gripping ability, while the talons are almost straight.

One of the most distinctive subfamilies of the Accipitridae is the Aegypiinae, or "Old World Vultures." They bear a close resemblance to the American New World Vultures, but their beaks are much more strongly hooked, while their round nostrils and syrinx (vocal organs) indicate they developed in more recent evolutionary times. Of this group, the Egyptian Vulture is the smallest, with a wing span of up to six feet; the Griffon Vulture (see text entry), by contrast, is twice its size.

In flight the Egyptian Vulture shows a distinctive flight silhouette, with long, straight-edged, pointed black, and white wings and a wedge-shaped white tail. A dirty-white-looking bird, closer views show its white feathers are tinged with varying shades of buff or dirty orange. The head is small and slim, covered with yellow skin and bordered by loose, scraggly feathers. The bill is slim and weak looking, and not so adept at tearing flesh as large vultures. The Egyptian Vulture breeds across southern europe and Asia Minor to India and over much of Africa. In Europe it is widely found in Spain, with scattered pockets of breeding birds in France, Italy, and the Balearics.

Totally migratory in Europe, it moves south of the Sahara, and many can be seen as they pass over the Straits of Gibraltar in spring and autumn. The Egyptian Vulture has had a long association with man and is frequently depicted in the art of the ancient Egyptians, who gave it the name of "Pharaoh's Chicken." One of the most interesting aspects of this species' feeding behavior is its habit of breaking ostrich eggs and those of other ground-nesting birds with nearby stones.

OUTLINE OF THE FALCONIDAE

Just as everyone can recognize a bird of prey in general, most can identify a falcon in particular. Though they vary in size from the rather large Gyr Falcon to the tiny falconets, they mostly share the long, rather pointed wings and sleek lines that distinguish them at a glance from other diurnal birds of prey. However, there are some that are less obviously falcons and to arrive at a more precise definition, ornithologists must refer to details of the skeleton, the pattern of moult, and biochemistry.

There are about sixty species in the family Falconidae, conventionally divided into four subfamilies. The first is the Micrasturinae, known as

forest falcons. These aberrant falcons live in the rain forests of Central and South America, from Mexico southward. Sometimes known as "harrier-hawks," they resemble a cross between a Hen Harrier and a Goshawk, with barred underparts, long tails, long legs, and a facial "ruff"—raised head feathers that may help to detect sound. Their habits are poorly known, beyond the fact that they live in dense forests and prey on birds, lizards, and invertebrates; at least one species has been seen following army ant trails, presumably to feed on the many small birds that attend the ants. There are five or six species of forest falcon, depending on which authority you choose to follow.

The second group is the Herpetotherinae, or Laughing Falcon. This subfamily contains just one species, *Herpetotheres cachinnans*, another Central and South American species. Also poorly known, it keeps watch from a treetop perch over areas of open ground and feeds on snakes and nests in tree cavities. The Laughing Falcon gets its name from its loud calls, and pairs will duet at dusk and dawn.

Thirdly, there are the Daptriinae, or caracaras, perhaps the most unfalconlike of all the falcons. These are large, long-legged and long-tailed birds that spend much time on the ground or loafing about; the name caracara comes from their harsh, cackling voices. Largely a South American group of nine species, one, the Guadalupe Caracara *Polyborus lutosus*), is now extinct. The best known is undoubtedly the Crested Caracara (*P. plancus*), which is found from Arizona, Texas, and Florida south through the Caribbean to Tierra del Fuego and the Falkland Islands at the extreme southern tip of South America. It is found in open bushland and, like other caracaras, often feeds on carrion, together with vultures. And, like vultures, it has areas of bare skin around the head in order to avoid soiling itself with the viscera of dead animals. It also feeds on small birds, insects, and even plant material. Inhabiting a wide range of habitats, from open country to forest, caracaras build their own nests, unlike other "falcons."

The fourth group is the subfamily Falconinae, or the true falcons. With about forty-seven species, it includes the most widespread and best known of the falcons. There are three genera of small falcons. The pygmy falcons, or falconets, are a group of eight species found only in the tropics. These are smallest diurnal raptors, with the White-fronted Falconet (*Microhierax latifrons*) of northern Borneo being the smallest of all. At a mere fifteen centimeters long and weighing just thirty-five grams, it is only very slightly larger than a sparrow. Perhaps the most familiar of these tiny falcons is, however, the Pygmy Falcon (*Polihierax semitorquatus*) of the dry bushland and savanna of East and South Africa. This breeds in the nests of various species of weaver and is often easy to spot as it sits on prominent perches on the tops of acacia trees. Like all these small falcons, it has rather shrikelike feeding habits, making short sallies from its perch to catch insects, whilst the other members of the group may also take small birds, mammals, and reptiles.

The bulk of the true falcons are placed in the genus *Falco*, comprised of thirty-nine species that everyone would recognize as falcons. They are found throughout the world, but their various aerial hunting techniques limit them to relatively open habitats with good visibility. True falcons are often stocky, with well-developed pectoral muscles, rather short tails, and long, pointed wings. They can be divided into several convenient groups, depending upon the type of prey sought and the hunting techniques used.

The largest falcons—including the Gyr (*F. rusticolus*), Saker (*F. cherrug*), and Prairie Falcon (*F. mexicanus*)—specialize in striking prey on or near the ground. They are the "ground-attack" members of the family, surprising ptarmigan or small mammals such as hamsters with a rapid, low-level flight, and knocking them down before they have a chance to escape. Due to their spectacular hunting techniques, they have always been popular with falconers. However, it is another species, the Peregrine Falcon (*F. peregrinus*), that has perhaps the most dramatic hunting technique of all. A cosmopolitan species, it is the "dive-bomber" of the bird world, specializing in taking larger birds, such as pigeons and ducks, in amazing "stoops," a near-vertical dive upon its prey at incredible speed. Not surprisingly, it too is a great favorite of falconers.

Another group of smaller falcons, including the hobbies and Merlin (*F. columbarius*), also catch birds in flight, but they favor smaller birds and also large insects and use their sheer speed and agility in level flight to bag their prey. Long-winged and very fast, they can even catch swifts on the wing. Closely similar are Eleonora's and Sooty Falcons (*F. eleonorae* and *F. concolor*, respectively). Both are found around the Mediterranean and Red Sea and are well adapted to prey on the millions of small birds that migrate from Europe and Asia to spend the winter in Africa. Indeed, so specialized are they that their autumn breeding season is timed to coincide with the peak of southward migration.

Closely related to the hobbies are the two forms of Red-footed Falcon (*F. vespertinus*) of eastern Europe and Asia. These are highly gregarious and feed largely on insects caught on the wing. They breed in colonies, taking over the nest of Rooks (*Corvus frugilegus*) once the Rook's own young have fledged. Also similar in habits is the Lesser Kestrel (*F. naumanni*) which, despite its mane and appearance, does not seem to be closely related to the other kestrels.

The kestrels themselves are a large group, including the Common Kestrel (*F. tinnunculus*) and American Kestrel (*F. sparverius*), perhaps the two most familiar birds of prey in Britain and North America, respectively. They all feed on insects and small mammals taken on the ground, many species hovering over one place in order to spot potential prey. The group includes the Mauritius Kestrel (*F. punctatus*), which is the rarest of the falcons, with only about a dozen pairs.

OUTLINE OF THE TYTONIDAE

The Tytonidae, or barn owls, is a small family of just seventeen species that includes on one of the most familiar and best-known owls in the world and some of the rarest and most enigmatic owls of all. Indeed, six species are listed in the latest International Council for Bird Preservation (ICBP) checklist of threatened birds.

Closely related to the typical owls, or Strigidae, the barn owls differ formerly only in minor details of the skeleton, particularly the breast bone. Nevertheless, to the birdwatcher, they are readily separated from other owls by their heart-shaped facial disk; all-dark eyes; long, slender legs with a comblike middle claw; and lack of ear tufts.

The family is divided into two genera. The genus *Tyto* includes the

Barn Owl (*T. alba*), the most widespread species, occurring in North and South America, Europe, Africa, Arabia, southern Asia, and Australia. Due to this wide distribution, the Barn Owl is one of the most familiar of all owls, a familiarity compounded by its habit of hunting during the daytime, especially during the winter and when feeding young, and its preference for rough grassland and field edges, which brings it into contact (sometimes fatally) with the motorist. In Britain and Europe, Barn Owls commonly roost and nest in ruined buildings, churches, and barns, and the association with such places, as well as the ghostly white appearance in flight, may have been a large factor in the association of owls in general with the supernatural.

Apart from the Barn Owl, two other members of the genus are relatively widespread, the two grass owls which, as their name suggests, are found in grasslands in Africa, India, and through the Philippines and Indonesia to Australia. Closely related, the African Grass Owl (*T. capensis*) is often treated as the same species as the Eastern Grass Owl (*T. longimembris*) of Asia and Australia. Grass owls roost by day in hollows or short tunnels in the grasslands, and if disturbed tend to fly short distances only. Favoring areas of rank vegetation, they are seldom seen unless disturbed (for example, by elephants on a tiger hunt) and are thus relatively poorly known.

The Barn Owl has a propensity to wander, and in the process has colonized many oceanic islands. Indeed, its adaptability has been demonstrated recently by its spread into Malaya. Formerly covered in rain forest, a habitat not favored by the Barn Owl, Malaya is now filled with oilpalm plantations, which has created a niche for the species to exploit; infested by rats, the Malayan plantation owners now positively encourage Barn Owls. Perhaps another product of this island-hopping ability is the development of several endemic island forms. One of these, the Ashy-faced Owl (*T. glaucops*) of Hispaniola in the Caribbean has recently been elevated to the status of a full species following the discovery that it breeds alongside Barn Owls on that island. Also notable is the fossil evidence for the existence of several other endemic barn owls on the West Indies, all now extinct, and the fact that there is increasing evidence that some of the birds currently thought to be island races of the Barn Owl may too be separate species.

The other members of the genus *Tyto* are mostly island endemics and are almost all forest birds. The Lesser Sooty Owl (*T. multipunctata*) and Masked Owl (*T. novaehollandiae*) are found in Australia and New Guinea, with the Greater Sooty Owl (*T. tenebricosa*) in eastern Australia only. The form of Masked Owl on Tasmania is so much larger than that of mainland Australia that it is often considered a separate species, Tasmanian Masked Owl (*T. castanops*). These owls prey on small mammals, such as possums, and, in the case of Masked Owls—which may be found in more open areas along the forest edge—on mammals, birds, and reptiles, including rabbits taken from traps. On the island of New Britain, off Papua New Guinea, the Golden Owl (*T. aurantia*) occurs in forest and has only been seen a few times, while the Manus Masked Owl (*T. manusi*) is endemic to Manus in the Admiralty Islands.

In Indonesia there are a further four barn owls. The Sulawesi Owl (*T. rosenbergii*) is thought to be closely related to the Masked Owl, but it occupies a wider variety of habitats, including cultivation in the vicini-

ty of human habitations. This wide habitat tolerance may be the reason that the Barn Owl is not found on Sulawesi, as it is "excluded" from its normal niche by the presence of the endemic Sulawesi Owl. However, another endemic barn owl is found on Sulawesi, the Minahassa Owl (*T. inexspectata*). This species was known from just nine specimens, but in the early 1980s one bird was caught and another seen in the northeast portion of the island. Not surprisingly, little is known about its habits, but presumably its preference for forest may prevent it from competing with the Sulawesi Owl. The Lesser Masked Owl (*T. sororcula*) is found on the island of Buru in the south Moluccas and in Tanninbar. Even more enigmatic than the Minahassa Owl, it is known from two specimens taken on Buru and two birds collected on Tanninbar. It is thought to inhabit forest, but has never been observed in the field. And, most mysterious of all is the Taliabu Owl (*T. nigrobrunnea*), known from a single specimen collected on Taliabu in the Sula islands off eastern Sulawesi. Another rare island barn owl is the Madagascar Red Owl (*T. soumagnei*). It is confined to the ever-declining rain forests of eastern Madagascar and has been seen just once since 1934, making it one of the rarest and most poorly known of the Madagascar endemics.

The second genus in the family Tytonidae is *Phodilus*, the bay owls. They differ from barn owls in having the facial disk incomplete above the eyes and a relatively weak bill, and their short wings and tail make them even better adapted to a closed environment than the various forest barn owls. There is one relatively widespread species, the Bay Owl (*P. badius*) of Sri Lanka, Indian, Southeast Asia, Borneo, Sumatra, and Java. Strictly nocturnal, it is found in rain forest and seldom seen, though it does give a variety of wailing screeches that enable it to be tracked down with perseverance. The second species in this group is another totally enigmatic and mysterious owl, the Congo Bay Owl (*P. prigoginei*). Known from a single female collected in eastern Zaire in 1951, it is an amazing example of a central African representative of an Asian group lying "hidden" in the Congo forests.

OUTLINE OF THE STRIGIDAE

Even to a nonbirdwatcher, owls are an immediately recognizable and easily identified group of birds. Their soft, usually intricately marked plumage makes them a thing of beauty, while the big head and forward-facing eyes set in a rounded facial disk, plus the ability to blink with the upper eyelid, give them an almost human expression.

The common characteristics that make owls so easily recognizable to humans are all adaptations to a very specialized way of life. Owls are basically nocturnal birds of prey, their common characteristic being that they hunt in the twilight or darkness (of course, there are some owls that hunt during the day, but these are nocturnal species that have adapted to a daytime schedule). At night two senses are paramount in securing their prey: sight and sound.

Their large eyes are an adaptation to see well at low light levels. The large retina has plenty of light-sensitive rods, but they still need some light to see; in total darkness, they are blind. Their closely set eyes give them excellent binocular vision, enabling them to pinpoint their prey. The eyes are relatively fixed, however, and hence an owl must turn its whole head to look sideways.

The dense, abundant plumage helps to keep the bird warm during long periods of inactivity between hunting forays, and the delicate, cryptic patterns keep it hidden from small birds during the daytime, who will scold and mob any owl they find. Yet, the most important factor about an owl's plumage is its specialized structure, which enables the bird to fly silently, approaching its prey without being detected. The sense of sound plays an important part in the hunting techniques of most owls. They have very acute hearing, and the facial disk may serve to enhance the ears' sound gathering abilities. This enables them to home-in on the rustles and squeaks of small mammals, in some cases even in absolute darkness. For many woodland and forest owls, detecting their prey by sound must be more important than sight, as light levels are so low in the forest at night.

The affinities of owls have been long debated. Ecologically, they are the nocturnal counterparts of the diurnal birds of prey, but are they closely related? The latest opinion is that owls are not hawks or falcons that have become adapted to hunting in the dark, but are related to nightjars, frogmouths, and potoos, having evolved from a common, nocturnal ancestor perhaps one hundred million years ago. Amazingly, their next closest cousins are thought to be the turacos and plantain-eaters of Africa.

All owls are placed in the order Strigiformes, and this is then divided into two groups, the typical owls of the family Strigidae and the barn owls of the family Tytonidae. Within the Strigidae itself, there are anywhere between 134 and 161 species, depending on which taxonomic authority one follows. This amalgam is further divided into twenty-three genera.

One of the most familiar groups of owls is the genus *Strix*, which includes the Tawny Owl (*S. aluco*) of Europe. Like the other seventeen members of the genus, which occur in North and South America, Africa, and Asia, it is a forest bird and strictly nocturnal. In Britain and Europe, the Tawny Owl has adapted to suburban habitats, and its eerie calls can be heard late at night in many parks and gardens. The exception to the preference for forests in this genus is Hume's Tawny Owl (*S. butleri*) of the deserts of the Middle East. This little-known owl breeds in remote arid wadis, using caves and crevices to nest in. Another genus of wood owls is *Asio*, the "eared" owls. Although mostly a forest bird, the Short-eared Owl (*A. flammeus*) is widely distributed in the Americas, Europe and Asia, and is a familiar due to its habitual daylight hunting over open ground, where it specializes in small mammals.

Another familiar genus is *Otus*, the scops-owls. It includes the Scops-Owl (*O. scops*) of southern Europe, where it is a familiar garden bird, giving its monotonous, electronic-sounding "toik" call being given for hours at a time. Also familiar are the two screech owls of North America, Western (*O. kennicottii*) and Eastern (*O. asio*). This pair illustrates a particular problem of owls in general, and scops-owls in particular. Having such a specialized way of life, they all look basically very similar, and it can be difficult to separate them into species based simply on appearance. Western and Eastern Screech Owls were only recognized as separate species when detailed studies of their vocalizations showed that

they overlapped in the Great Plains. It is studies of voice, too, that have elucidated the difficult taxonomy of scops-owls in other parts of the world. Basically forest birds, they occur throughout North and South America, Africa, and Asia, but reach their maximum diversity in the islands of the Philippines, Malaysia, and Indonesia. About fifty-three species of scops-owl are currently recognized.

Connected with this great diversity, scops-owls also have another notable characteristic, the ability to colonize oceanic islands. No less than twenty-two species are found on single islands or island groups, and one species, Moluccan Scops-Owl (*O. magicus*) has a far-flung distribution encompassing the Seychelles, Indonesia, and New Guinea. Clearly, like rails, pigeons, and white-eyes, their abilities in the field of overwater flight should not be underestimated. Though not closely related, the Boreal or Tengmalm's Owl (*Aegolius funereus*) and saw-whet owls (*Aegolius*) share many of the scops-owls' habits.

Another genus to specialize in island-hopping is *Ninox*, the hawk-owls or boobook owls. With eighteen species in the Oriental and Australasian region, they have their highest diversity in Australasia and the islands off New Guinea. The most familiar, however, is the Brown Hawk-Owl (*N. scutulata*), which has a range stretching from India to Japan and south to Java. They are all characterized by a reduction in the facial disk, having a smaller and more rounded head than other owls. This, and a tendency to have longer and narrower wings and a longer tail, are presumably convergent with diurnal birds of prey. Hawk-owls hunt mostly at dusk and dawn and rely largely on sight alone to detect their prey. The Hawk-Owl (*Surnia ulula*) of the taiga zone right round the Northern Hemisphere is not closely related but is similar in shape and structure.

Another group of owls that sometimes hunt by day are the pygmy-owls (*Glaucidium*), with a total twenty species; elf owl (*Micrathene whitneyi*), Burrowing Owl (*Speotyto cunicularia*), and the three little owls of *Athene*. The American Northern Pygmy Owl (*G. gnoma*) is perhaps the best known of the group. Despite the fact that most species feed on rodents and invertebrates, they are feared by small birds, and a bird-watcher in Africa can often elicit an excited response from otherwise peaceful birds by imitating the whistle of a Pearl-spotted Owlet (*G. perlatum*).

At the other end of the scale from the pygmy-owls are the eagle-owls, *Bubo*, a group of fourteen species that specialize in very large prey. Their prominent ear tufts have, in fact, nothing to do with hearing, but are rather used to signal the bird's mood. The Great Horned Owl (*B. virginianus*) of North America is perhaps the most familiar. It feeds on birds up to the size of a pheasant and mammals up to the size of a rabbit. It occupies a range of habitats, from the taiga forest to tropical rain forest and mangroves, and this adaptability is shared by the whole genus. Specialized offshoots of the eagle-owls are the fishing owls *Scotopelia* and *Ketupa* of Africa and Asia. They have abandoned the specialized adaptations needed to fly silently, presumably because fish cannot hear their aerial approach, and they have featherless feet, adapted to grip a slippery fish. Another dramatic relative of the eagle-owls is the Snowy Owl (*Nyctea scandiaca*), which occurs on the tundra of the high Arctic.

FEEDING BIOLOGY

Birds of prey are faced with a fundamental problem. Not surprisingly, their prey, whether it be other birds, mammals, or insects, does not want to be caught and eaten. Further, these other animals have developed a bewildering variety of strategies to avoid just that fate, from camouflage, armor, and nocturnal habits to acute senses of hearing, sight, and smell. To these strategies birds of prey have had to respond with their own adaptations, to overcome the preys' defenses and get themselves a meal. On top of this, they have also had to develop methods of catching, holding, and killing their prey.

Perhaps the most obvious physical attribute of all birds of prey is their hooked bill. Beyond this simple similarity there is a wealth of detail, designed to deal with particular prey. The huge, shearing bill of a Black Vulture is the perfect tool to cut through the tough hides of dead large animals, while the hooked bill of many other birds of prey is designed to pull apart their prey once it has been caught. Most raptors kill with their feet, and it is only the falcons, which have a distinct notch in the cutting edge of the bill (designed to sever the spinal chord of small birds and mammals), and some of the kites (which are similarly equipped to deal with lizards and large invertebrates) that habitually use their bill as a killing weapon.

It is thus the feet that are dangerous, and birds of prey have a wide variety of feet, adapted to their particular hunting methods. Vultures, which do not hunt at all, have heavy feet and claws, ideal for shambling along the ground and coping in the fray (were they to have razor-sharp claws, they would inflict too many injuries on each other in the melee around a carcass). Most other raptors have talons with strong, curved, and razor-sharp claws, designed to grab their prey and hold it securely. There are further specializations, however. Raptors that feed on fish, such as the Osprey and various sea- and fish-eagles, need to be able to grab and clasp their slippery prey, and to this end have small spikes, or "spicules," on the soles of their feet. Many of the smaller eagles specialize in snakes, and their legs have a tough armor of imbricated scales, in order to protect themselves from poisonous bites. The various species of harriers, which feed on small birds and mammals caught in long, rough grassland, crops, and reedbeds, have extraordinarily long legs, to enable them to pounce on their prey in the vegetation.

Birds of prey have developed very acute sight and vision, having in particular perhaps the sharpest sight of any birds. They have relatively large eyes (in some species as large as a man's), which produce a large image on the retina, which in turn has a large number of cones and optic nerve fibers in order to detect a detailed image and transmit it in code to the brain. Some raptors are thought to have up to eight times the visual acuity of man, though three times the acuity may be a more realistic estimate. Visual acuity, that is the ability to distinguish fine detail, should not be confused with visual sensitivity, the ability to detect small quantities of light. The structural adaptations for these two purposes cannot be accommodated easily in the same eye, and thus a bird can rarely excel at both. Not surprisingly, all owls have excellent vision in low light levels, but their sight is not that acute. Thus, like some other birds of prey, they largely depend on their hearing to locate their prey.

All birds of prey have excellent hearing, but it is particularly well developed in the owls and in some raptors that hunt in closed environments, such as forests, or where it is difficult to spot their prey. Experiments have shown that some owls can catch prey in total darkness, using sound alone. In order to achieve such accuracy, the holes for each ear are of slightly different sizes and shapes and are in a slightly different position on the head; this asymmetry allows an accurate audio picture to be built up. Most owls also have a facial disk, which is thought to enhance their sense of hearing, and the forest-falcons of South America and the various harriers also have a ruff or facial disk that may serve a similar purpose. The forest falcons are crepuscular, hunting in the forest twilight, and harriers hunt over rough grass, where small rodents may be more easily heard than seen.

One final sense must be mentioned, the sense of smell. In most birds this is very poor, but in three species of New World vulture, the Turkey Vulture and the two yellow-headed vultures, it is well developed. They can detect a hidden carcass by scent alone and are even able to tell how rotten the carcass is by its smell.

Having located its prey, and with the equipment to effectively grab and dispatch the unfortunate victim, raptors still have to catch the sparrow, mouse, or snake concerned. To do this, they use three basic techniques, and their wings, as the method of locomotion, are adapted accordingly.

The first and most dramatic method is to overwhelm the victim with sheer speed. This is the technique used by many falcons, with the past master being the Peregrine Falcon. A Peregrine will cruise over a suitable area, and when it spots a potential victim, such as a duck, wader or Wood Pigeon, it launches into a steep dive, or "stoop," with the wings half closed, in which it may attain a speed of 112 miles per hour (and even 224 miles per hour has been suggested for the fastest stoop, though this figure is doubtful). Falcons have long, pointed wings, designed for great speed in level and diving flight.

The second method is to surprise the prey, approaching unseen and catching it before it has a chance to escape. A typical example is the Sparrowhawk, which will fly fast and low along the line of a hedge, occasionally jinking from one side of bushes to the other, hoping to surprise small birds. Sparrowhawks and other members of the genus *Accipiter* have relatively short, broad wings, designed for maneuverability at low speeds.

The third method is to pounce on the prey from above. Many raptors, such as Buzzards, will soar over an area, surveying the ground below, and then dropping on a rabbit or other small mammal when they spot it from the air. They have long, broad wings, well suited to hours of soaring flight with a very low expenditure of energy. A variation is to hover over an area of suitable habitat, keeping the head still and surveying the ground to spot mice or voles in the grass. This is typified by the Kestrel. A third variation is to use a perch as a lookout post in a "wait and see" technique, dropping onto the prey once seen or heard. This is favored by many owls, such as the Tawny Owl.

Of course, there are other variations in hunting techniques, from vultures, who soar at a great height over the ground, using their very keen eyesight to spot the carcasses of dead animals (and also watching other vultures, in case they spot the food first), to the Secretary Bird, which stalks the plains of Africa on foot, snatching up lizards, snakes, small rodents, and young birds.

BREEDING BIOLOGY

Not surprisingly, for such a large and varied group as the birds of prey, a wide variety of breeding strategies are employed. Of course, the first step in the process of procreation is to attract a mate and to establish the pair bond.

To attract a mate, raptors, like most other birds, use a variety of advertisement displays. At it simplest form this involves the bird sitting on a tree, rock, or other prominent perch and calling loudly. Of course, no bird of prey has anything approaching the elaborate songs of the Passerines or perching birds, but their calls in this case fulfil the same function as a song. In the various diurnal birds of prey that live in woodland or forest, these vocal signals may be more important that any visual signals, as it is easier to hear another bird than to see it. This is taken to its logical conclusion in the nocturnal birds of prey, the owls. At night, visual signals can play little part in communication between individuals, and many owls have relatively elaborate vocalizations.

The next step onward from a purely vocal advertising display is to combine sight and sound. Many raptors will fly over their territory,

either soaring in wide circles or flying in a straight line, calling at intervals. Once the bird is in the air, however, the process of sexual selection (whereby the female selects the male that shows the most prowess in courtship, either with the most energetic display or the most elaborate ornamentations) would tend to push the advertisement display toward a more elaborate and acrobatic form.

The simple form of aerial display is an undulating flight. Undulations may be steep or shallow, the displaying bird diving downward fifty to one thousand feet before climbing upward again; depending on the species, the climb may require vigorous flapping. The undulations may be repeated many times, and this basic theme is elaborated in some species. For example, Tawny Eagles dive in a series of "pot-hooks," merely leveling out, rather than climbing, at the end of each dive, and thus losing height in a series of steps. Verreaux's Eagle, on the other hand, dives repeatedly in a series of "pendulum" swings, diving from side to side over the same course.

Such aerial displays may be used initially to attract a mate, but are repeated throughout the breeding season, and often throughout the year, serving to reinforce the pair bond, and often involve both sexes. The most commonly seen of these joint displays is when the male and female are soaring together over the territory, and then the male dives down on the female, who at the last moment rolls in flight to present her talons to the male. In the more spectacular variations, such those of the smaller hawk-eagles, the birds actually clasp talons and roll in a cartwheel, finally separating close to the ground.

Having met and courted, the pair needs a safe place to lay the eggs and raise the young—the nest. To meet this basic requirement, however, a wide variety of nests are used by raptors, from a mere scrape on a bare cliff ledge to some of the largest and most elaborate of any bird. Details of some of the variations will be found in the species accounts, and only the general trends will be mentioned here.

The nest is located in a suitable area for that particular species, with an adequate food supply, and not too close to the nest of another pair of the same species (even in colonially nesting raptors, such as Griffon Vultures, there is a minimum critical distance between each nest). It is the female that usually makes the final nest site selection, and in those species that build nests, the female also does the bulk of the construction work, although the male may provide much of the raw material. The nest may be built over the space of a few days in those species in temperate areas for which time is at a premium, to several months in the tropics where a more leisurely pace is possible. Even within the same species, this variation in timing between high and low latitudes may be seen. A new nest may be built each year, but some species use the same nest from year to year, making appropriate repairs, or a series of nests may be repaired and used in rotation.

For the New World vultures, falcons, and most owls, no nest is constructed at all—they take over the abandoned nests of other species or use a bare scrape, a rock crevice, or a hole in a tree. Of the species that construct nests themselves, a very wide variety of nests and nest sites are used. Most are built in trees, less often on cliffs and crags, and occasionally on the ground, though in the absence of suitable trees or cliffs a range of raptors have been recorded nesting on the ground, and the various harriers do so almost exclusively.

Just as the nests of birds of prey are varied, so are the eggs. They may be unmarked white, green-white or blue-white, or marked with shades of red, brown, and gray. In the falcons, the eggs are heavily marked with shades of red and are some of the most attractive of any bird eggs. The variety and beauty of the eggs of birds of prey has proved something of a disadvantage in some European countries, where they prove an irresistible draw to egg collectors, despite the illegality of this fascination.

Most diurnal raptors lay clutches of less than three eggs, with four to six being less common and found in the smaller birds of prey only. Among the owls, clutch size may vary with food supply, with arctic species, such as the Snowy Owl, laying up to fourteen eggs in years of an abundance. Conversely, when food is short, no eggs at all may be laid.

Eggs are laid at daily intervals, and often longer, so that in species with a large clutch there may be a gap of over ten days between the first and last eggs. Incubation periods are often long, in the larger birds being over fifty days, and in most species only the female incubates. She begins with the first or second egg, and this usually results in the eggs hatching in a staggered sequence. Consequently there are marked differences in the size of the young throughout the period of their development. In years of good food supply, all the young may survive, while in a bad year the older chicks compete with their younger siblings for food, and being larger and stronger survive while the younger chicks starve. This strategy may seem cruel, but it maximizes the number of young fledged in a good year while reducing the risk of total failure in a bad year.

Young birds of prey are helpless when they hatch, and are entirely dependent on the parents. They are covered with down and are brooded almost continually. After a few days the chick may move around the nest on its tarsi, and in many species competition now develops between the older and younger chick, especially in those that lay just two eggs. After a period, the first coat of down is replaced by a second, thicker and warmer coat. Despite its better protection, the chick is still frequently brooded, especially at night. Between a third and a half of the way through the fledging period the first true feathers start to appear on the wings and tail. At this stage the young are able to stand and walk around the nest; once fully feathered, they may be left alone on the nest for most of the day. They can now feed themselves, and no longer beg for food, grabbing it from the adult, and they may exhibit threat postures rather than the submissive begging positions of younger chicks.

The fledging periods of raptors are as varied as incubation periods, and vary largely with the size of the bird, being about three weeks for the smaller falcons to over three months in some of the larger tropical eagles and vultures. When almost ready to leave the nest, the chicks will begin to exercise their wings vigorously, especially on windy days in those species that do not nest in holds or crevices. The first real flight is a spontaneous decision of the chick, usually without any coaxing from the adults. It may fly some distance before alighting rather clumsily on a tree or on the ground. However, they quickly learn adequate flying skills, though they continue to be dependent on the adults for some time after leaving the nest as they learn hunting skills.

HABITATS AND POPULATIONS

Birds of prey are, by definition, predators. And, as predators, are totally dependent for survival upon their prey. There are, of course, exceptions to this strict definition, especially those raptors that are scavengers rather than hunters. Yet even scavengers are dependent upon prey species; they merely wait for something other than themselves to kill it (whether it be accident, old age, illness, or other predators). The flip side of this predator-prey relationship is that wherever there is suitable prey, from insects and other invertebrates to mammals and birds, there will be birds of prey.

Every land habitat from the arctic tundra to tropical rain forest is inhabited by raptors. We have to say land habitat, for they have never succeeded in exploiting the oceans. Of course, a few birds—such as sea eagles, fish eagles, kites, and the Osprey—are to be found along the seashore, but all are very strictly tied to the land to sleep and breed, and could not survive more than a few hours at sea. There is one other place that raptors have never colonized: the Antarctic. Despite the seasonal abundance of food around the various seabird and mammal colonies, with no resident land mammals or birds, the winters are just too long and bleak to allow any raptor to survive.

Birds of prey are thus near universal in their distribution on land, but just as there is a great variety of habitats, there is a great variety in bird of prey communities. Some habitats are simple, with relatively few "niches" for raptors (that is, few sources of food available for exploitation). Perhaps the simplest of all is the arctic tundra, where throughout the animal and plant kingdom, simplicity is the rule. There are relatively few species of insect, bird, and mammal to feed on (though those that are present may be superabundant). Thus, there are relatively few raptor species present, though those that are there may be rather common. Rough-legged Buzzard, Peregrine, Gyr Falcon, and Snowy Owl are the typical species found in arctic regions, and all four are found throughout the Northern Hemisphere, from Scandinavia through Siberia to Alaska, arctic Canada, and Greenland.

Like many simple systems, the arctic ecology is easily unbalanced, and many species go through cycles of boom and bust. The most famous of these is, of course, the lemming cycle, usually of around four years, and those raptors that have lemmings as their principal foods go through similar cycles. This is particularly true of Rough-legged Buzzards and Snowy Owls and illustrates the price to be paid for dependence on a limited range of prey species.

At the other extreme, tropical rain forests provide a complex habitat with a large number of niches available, as there are many different prey species, each requiring different techniques and specializations on the part of the predator. Insects and other invertebrates, small birds and mammals, and even large birds and mammals, such as monkeys, provide a food source for raptors. Indeed, some of the largest birds of prey are the Philippine Eagle and Harpy Eagle, both forest species that feed on monkeys.

In tropical forests, there is often a wide range of raptor species, but each one usually occurs at low densities. This is because the available food resources are divided up among so many niches that each can only support a relatively low population. However, because of the complexity of the system, it is relatively stable, and the populations of each species are unlikely to fluctuate very much.

Despite their variety, tropical forest raptors are often difficult to see. They may sit quietly for long periods, or hunt unseen above the canopy. This is not the case with the raptors of another special habitat, perhaps the richest in the World, the savannas of Africa. It is not surprising that a continent that supports the largest and most varied mammal fauna in the world should also support a large number and variety of raptors, for where there is prey, there will be predators. It is perhaps the ease with which birds of prey can be seen in much of Africa that is the important factor, however, for with open vistas birds may be seen at long range, or easily spotted in the open, whereas in a forest habitat, they would be well hidden.

Moving onto more mundane places, the well-ordered farmland and woodland of much of Europe and North America supports an artificially limited variety of hawks, falcons, and owls. This is because of a three-pronged attack on raptor populations by man. First, by limiting the prey available, we limit the predators. There is no room for large or destructive mammals in the modern world, nor for so-called pest species. Second, through the insidious effects of various farm chemicals, industrial waste, and other toxins, the populations of some species of birds of prey may be kept artificially low. Third, raptors are directly attacked by man. They are killed because of their perceived competition for game species, such as pheasant, grouse or fish. Their eggs are stolen by "collectors"; and eggs and chicks are being stolen by advocates of the medieval art of falconry.

Despite the odds against them, some birds of prey are to be found in farmland, and even in towns and cities. They tend to be the smaller species, which feed on small mammals and birds. For example, in Britain the Kestrel, Sparrowhawk, and Tawny Owl have all thrived, as their particular niche is still available, and they may even benefit from reduced competition with other raptors.

MIGRATION AND MOVEMENTS

Of all the aspects of bird of prey behavior, it is perhaps their migrations that hold the greatest fascination for birdwatchers, have consequently attracted much study, and yet still hold the greatest mystique. Two factors combine to make the migrations of many raptors an ornithological spectacle. First, they are largely diurnal migrants, especially the larger species. Thus, unlike the unseen high-flying songbirds, their movements have been observed by man since the dawn of history. Second, they congregate in very large numbers at certain favored locations, enhancing the spectacle.

Like most birds, raptors migrate in response to fluctuations in their food supply. It is not necessarily cold weather or drought per se that forces them to move; rather it is a shortage of suitable prey. And, for those species for which suitable prey is still available, staying put, even in arctic conditions, is a better strategy for survival than risking the rigors of migration. Thus, in the Arctic, several species of owl endure hard winters so long as a supply of voles and lemmings is available.

Species from Europe, Asia, and North America that do migrate are not only those that feed on clearly seasonal prey—such as Swainson's and Broad-winged Hawks, Honey Buzzards, and the smaller, insect-eating falcons—but also larger birds, such as harriers, Steppe Eagles, and Ospreys, which would seem to have a less vulnerable food supply. Yet, over much of continental America and Eurasia, the winters are so severe as to make all but those species that feed on the hardiest prey desert the region.

In the tropics too, the variation between the wet and dry season may be just as pronounced as between summer and winter, and many birds will migrate, following the rains. In Africa Swallow-tailed Kite and Black Kite, for example, perform inter tropical migrations, and in South America the Plumbeous Kite does likewise. Diurnal birds of prey migrate entirely during the day and can be divided into two groups according to their travel method. First are the soaring species, which use an energy-efficient gliding and soaring flight, and second are the falcons and accipiters, which use a more active flight but which are less dependent on topography and geography in determining their migration routes.

Many of the larger broad-winged birds of prey employ the soaring method. They gain height on the thermals produced by the sun heating the ground, or the updrafts produced by cliffs and escarpments, and then glide for many miles, gradually loosing height, until they are forced to find another thermal. This method requires remarkably little energy (and many species do not feed on migration), but puts the birds at the mercy of the weather, as a favorable wind is necessary. It also dictates the routes that they can follow; most importantly, thermals do not develop over open water, so many species are forced to undertake long detours to avoid water crossings.

Much study in Europe, Asia, and Africa has begun to reveal the routes taken by migrating raptors. The Mediterranean forms a great barrier and most species avoid it. In the west, the straits of Gibraltar form a convenient crossing point, where a single glide can take a bird from Europe to Africa. However, a far larger number of birds breed in Eastern Europe and Asia, and these are concentrated at the eastern end of the Mediterranean, but here the Black and Caspian seas, as well as a variety of mountain ranges, form a complex of barriers to migrating birds of prey. Some cross from Europe to Asia at the Bosphorus, sailing over the rooftops of Istanbul. Other, lesser-known routes are through eastern Turkey, the Caucasus passes between Russia and Georgia, and around the southeast corner of the Caspian Sea; for example, nearly one hundred and forty thousand Honey Buzzards have been logged moving south in eastern Turkey in a single autumn. In North America, Hawk Mountain in Pennsylvania is a famous raptor watch point, though the concentrations here are small when compared with those farther south.

The greatest spectacle of migration is to be found at the point where birds can move easily from one continent to another, from Asia to Africa or from North to South America. In southern Israel at the seaside resort of Eilat up to 1,200,000 birds of prey have been counted in a spring season, and in the little-known country of Djibouti, over seventy-five thousand Steppe Eagles have been logged in a single autumn crossing from Arabia to Africa. And, in the New World, between three hundred thousand and seven hundred thousand each of Swainson's Hawks, Broad-winged Hawks, and Turkey Vultures pass through Panama en route from North to South America.

Many of the smaller birds of prey, such as falcons, accipiters, and harriers, use a more active flight on migration. They are able to make relatively long sea crossings and are thus not concentrated at certain points in the same way as the large species. Perhaps the most spectacular examples are Eleonora's and Sooty Falcons, which winter in Madagascar, and Eastern Red-footed Falcons, which cross the Indian Ocean en route from eastern Asia to winter quarters in Africa. However, many of these smaller raptors still prefer an easy life where possible, and numbers may be seen at certain favored passes, taking the easiest route across the mountains. They also differ from the larger species in that they are able to hunt en route.

Because of their mobility and capacity to fast—many species of raptors can go several days without feeding—birds of prey do not only undertake regular migrations, they also have less predictable wanderings, where they move in response to local fluctuations in the food supply. This is especially pronounced at northern latitudes, involving owls and Rough-legged Buzzards, and in the tropics, where locust swarms of areas of grass fires may attract hundreds of insectivorous birds of prey.

The arctic ecosystem is relatively simple and also relatively unstable, and many animals undergo marked fluctuations in abundance. As previously mentioned, the most famous of these is the lemming cycle, which has a roughly four-year rotation, and the birds of prey that prey on lemmings fluctuate in parallel with their prey. In the years that the rodent population crashes, species such as Snowy, Great Gray, and Tengmalm's Owls and Rough-legged Buzzards move south in search of food. The more pronounced of these irregular movements are known as "irruptions," and in irruption years such northern species may appear well to the south of the usual range, to the delight of birdwatchers.

SOCIAL BEHAVIOR

Birds of prey are not, by and large, social animals. Indeed, it is safe to say that they are rather solitary creatures, with few social interactions. In nature, little happens without a good reason, and two reasons may be advanced for the solitary nature of most raptors. First, their prey does not usually occur in such abundance that they can happily be shared with others of the same species—other groups of bird will often occur in flocks where there is a superabundance of food, such as swarming insects or spilled grain. Additionally, raptors do not need to be in a flock as a defense against predators—for many other species, the disadvantages of having to share a food resource are outweighed by the protection that being one of a multitude gives; in a flock, the chances are that it will be one of the *other* birds that is taken by a hawk or falcon. Although birds of prey do have predators themselves (and the smaller raptors may fall victim to the larger species), by and large they have little to worry about, apart from man and other mammalian hunters.

Not having any great reason to be social, most raptors are territorial, in that they defend a particular area of space. "Territories" can be divided into several categories. First, there is a nesting territory, which can range from just a few square yards of cliff ledge in the case of some of the colonial Old World vultures to a vast area into which no other bird of prey of any species is permitted to enter without being attacked. In general, however, a nesting territory will be defended against birds of the same species, and rather less often against other species of raptors.

The second type of territory occupied by birds of prey is the home range, which is the entire area used for feeding, nesting, recreation, roosting, and the like by an individual or pair. A home range is usually rather larger than the nesting territory and may well overlap with the home range of adjacent birds. The main point is that the home range, unlike the smaller nesting territory, is not actively defended, and birds from overlapping home ranges may meet without friction. This would not be possible if a neighbor strayed into the nesting territory, from which it would usually be vigorously driven off. There are variations, with some species, such as the African Fish Eagle, not defending a nesting territory at all. Other raptors will not tolerate a neighbor in any part of the home range; generally, these are the smaller raptors with smaller home ranges.

Raptors hold a territory for a variety of reasons. It may be to guarantee an adequate food supply, both for the adult birds and, during the breeding season, for the nestlings. It may also be an integral part of maintaining the bond between the sexes; fidelity is ensured by driving any potential rival from the area.

Many "resident" birds of prey wander during the nonbreeding season, and these and all migratory birds desert the nesting territory and home range during the winter. Some migrants become social during the nonbreeding season. Examples are Swainson's Hawk in the New World and various kites, eagles, and falcons in the Old. Some of these roost socially—such as the various harriers, Black Kites, and Merlins—dispersing during the day to become solitary hunters, while others—such as Lesser Kestrel and Red-footed Falcon—will both roost and hunt socially (notably, these are species that feed largely on large flying insects, such as locusts, which may be found in superabundant concentrations). Many birds of prey however, establish temporary winter food territories, which may be maintained for a period of a few days to a few months. These territories may not be actively defended, but nevertheless the individual birds apparently prefer to avoid each other. This may make good sense, for while the available food supply in a given area may be sufficient to support just one individual, if two attempt to exploit it, each will have to spend more time and energy finding food than is economical.

Having said that raptors are largely solitary, we have already introduced exceptions to this rule. Those birds of prey that are social for all or part of the year often exploit food sources that may be locally abundant. The small insectivorous falcons serve as examples, as do some of the Old World vultures. When a vulture finds a carcass, it cannot possibly eat all the carrion itself. A large animal would be sufficient for many meals, and as a vulture is not able to carry it off to a place of safety, long before it has a chance to consume the whole carcass it will have been found and stripped bare by other scavengers. Thus, Griffon Vultures hunt socially. They leave their cliff-ledge roosts in the early morning and spread out to cover a large area. Each bird watches not only the ground below, but each of the other vultures. When one finds a carcass, all of them can quickly move in to exploit it. Griffon Vultures not only hunt communally, they also breed and roost communally, and colonial nesting is also found in the social falcons.

Another exception is that many birds of prey will migrate in flocks. Many species of raptor do not feed on migration. For example, Steppe Eagles from central Asia will migrate to Africa without taking a meal. This clearly removes competition for food, and in these circumstances the benefits of flocking may overtake the drawbacks. Some of the larger birds of prey may migrate in flocks almost by accident. Most prefer to conserve energy by using a soaring and gliding flight, avoiding water crossings. Thus at various strategic bottlenecks, they will be concentrated in large numbers. In the case of some species, however, it is not convenience that draws a flock together. The Levant Sparrowhawk, for example, migrates in flocks of tens, hundreds, or even thousands of birds, the flocks being dense and tightly packed.

BIRDS OF PREY AND THEIR PLACE IN THE MODERN WORLD

More than any other group, birds of prey have suffered at the hand of man over the years, and the populations of many species are in decline. Indeed, thirty-eight species of hawk and falcon and a further twenty-one species of owl are treated as threatened by the ICBP. For every species, a detailed case history has been documented, but the threats fall into a few, clearly defined categories.

Mankind tends not to look favorably on other predators, and certainly not on birds of prey. Accused of killing pheasants, partridges, grouse, and other game species, birds of prey were for many years killed on the spot by gamekeepers. Happily, this is no longer the case, not least because of the decline of the great estates. But, of those keepers that remain, a substantial number still persecute birds of prey, despite the illegality of this practice in most countries. Farmers, too, are wary of their reputations as hunters, and especially in sheep country, Golden Eagles, Buzzards, and Red Kites are still killed with deliberately set poison baits.

When not persecuted because of a perceived competition with man, raptors may be hunted for sport. Especially in the Mediterranean countries, Ospreys, Honey Buzzards, and other soaring species are shot in some numbers. In the Third World, species such as the New Guinea Harpy Eagle may be hunted for their feathers, and owls, often thought of as birds of ill omen, may be killed on sight. Another "sport" that is particular threat in Britain and Germany is egg collecting. A minority of egg collectors consider it a great challenge to take the eggs of protected birds of prey, and these may change hands at high prices.

Birds of prey have a long association with man and have long been used in the noble art of falconry. Like egg collectors, a small minority of unscrupulous falconers in Europe and America rise to the challenge of stealing the eggs or young of protected species, but a much greater threat is posed to the populations of larger falcons in North Africa, the Middle East, and India, where falconry is a popular pastime with the elite of the various nations and tremendous prices may be paid for young Saker, Lanners, and Peregrines.

Another threat is a byproduct of modern agricultural methods and industrial waste. Birds of prey are at the top of the food chain. To take a simple example, sunlight gives plants the energy to grow, insects feed on the plants, small birds feed on the insects, and Sparrowhawks feed on the small birds. With the death of the Sparrowhawk, its body is returned to a lower stage in the food chain, as it is either decomposed by bacteria and the nutrients returned to the soil, or consumed by maggots and other insects. Being at the top of the food chain means that any toxic substances are concentrated in the bodies of birds of prey, and the effects of even minute traces of poisons in the environment can be magnified, often sufficiently to kill the raptor concerned.

In the late 1950s and early 1960s the widespread use of various pesticides, such as Dieldrin and DDT, led to population crashes in many species of raptor in Western Europe and North America. Peregrines, Sparrowhawks, and many other species became extremely scarce. Not only were the adult birds dying of poisoning, but also the pesticides concerned caused thinning of their eggshells, so that eggs were easily broken by accident during incubation. Gradually, as the effects of these toxic chemicals were realized, they were withdrawn from use and many of the species concerned have recovered, so much so that in Britain both Sparrowhawk and Peregrine are as numerous as they were before the introduction of these pesticides. Other, more insidious chemicals have now entered the environment, however, and we have yet to learn to full cost of their use. And, the pesticides that have now been banned in many industrialized countries are now being used in the Third World, resulting in population crashes of many raptors in those countries.

The final and most important threat to birds of prey is indirect. It is the destruction of their habitats, and consequently the removal of their

prey, nesting sites, and resting places. Of all the birds of prey considered threatened by the ICBP, only the Californian Condor, White-tailed Eagle, and Black Vulture are primarily at risk from persecution or pesticides. All the other species are threatened by habitat destruction—deforestation and the transformation of grasslands into agricultural land. The greater number of birds of prey are forest species and, as is well known, the destruction of tropical forest has caused a massive reduction in available habitat in the last fifty years. Species such as the Philippine (or Monkey-eating) Eagle, Madagascar Fish-Eagle, and Harpy Eagle are all threatened by the removal of their habitat, and even in the temperate zone, the exploitation of forests can put a bird at risk, such as the Spotted Owl of western North America.

Despite the fact that few birds of prey are at immediate risk of extinction from pesticides and persecution, these factors have played a major part in determining their place in the modern world. Most birdwatchers live in industrialized, intensively farmed countries, and in these areas the variety of raptors that one can expect to see on a normal day in the countryside has been shaped over the last two hundred years by farming methods and the use of chemicals, as well as direct persecution. And, looking back in time, the destruction of the temperate forests of Europe and North America, and the removal of a fauna of larger animals has also affected the spectrum of birds of prey that we can now watch.

Being spectacular, dramatic, and often large birds, raptors attract a lot of attention and often serve as "flagship species" for conservationists. In Britain the return of the Osprey, and in the United States the fate of the California Condor have attracted much public attention and interest. To conserve birds of prey, remembering that they are at the top of the food chain, it is necessary to save entire ecosystems and environments, and thus if we care enough about the fate of Peregrines, Golden Eagles, and Ospreys, we can also save the wild places that they need to live.

The contrasting, two-toned wings of silver gray flight feathers with black linings help to identify the Turkey Vulture as it sweeps majestically overhead in its constant search for prey.

1. SCAVENGERS OF THE BIRD WORLD

TURKEY VULTURE *CATHARTES AURA*

A classic example of the New World Vultures, of which there are seven species, the Turkey Vulture or Turkey Buzzard as it is colloquially known is a common sight over its range in North and South America. A highly migratory species, it moves north or south as the season dictates, often in flocks of several hundreds. At other times it might be seen singly or in small groups, as it seeks its prey coming together when food is located.

A large brown bird with a wing span of some six feet, it is an impressive sight as it wheels and soars without any apparent movement of the wings, these held at an angle above the horizontal. The similar Black Vulture, on the other hand, with which it often associates, flaps its wings more and soars with wings held horizontally.

Like Old World Vultures it is basically a carrion feeder, certainly in the northern parts of its range, but it does at times take young domestic animals. In southern parts of the range it is less of a scavenger, taking more live prey, such as birds or large insects.

It has long been argued that some carrion feeders find food as much by smell as by sight, and there is certainly evidence the Turkey Vulture does just that. It has been found that this species possesses one of the largest sets of olfactory organs of all birds, which indicates it has a keen sense of smell.

A Turkey Vulture's flight is quite distinctive, with the wings often held in a shallow "V." It also rocks from side to side, rarely flapping its wings. The long tail extends beyond the legs and feet when in flight.

A group of Turkey Vultures are shown perched on a tree. The two lower ones sit with their wings partly opened, apparently warming themselves in the sun, a behavior quite frequently observed in this species.

The California Condor is no longer to be seen in the skies above the Californian mountain ranges that were once its home. Reduced to a mere handful over the last fifty years, the remaining few birds have been taken into captivity in an attempt to save this magnificent bird of prey from extinction.

Silhouetted against an evening sky, a group of Black Vultures roosts in a dead tree in a Florida park. Confined more to the southern United States as a breeding bird, it is inclined not to wander as far afield in winter as the Turkey Vulture.

CALIFORNIA CONDOR *GYMNOGYPS CALIFORNIANUS*

North America's largest bird and the second largest bird of prey in the world, the adult male California Condor has a wing span of between nine and ten feet. The male is slightly larger than the female. Like most vultures it could be considered an ugly-looking creature. This species has a bald orange to grayish yellow head fading to light gray on the neck. There is a purplish patch on the side of the neck, and a small red wattle hangs from below the crop.

A ruff of long scraggly feathers encircles the neck, while the overall black plumage has a washed-out appearance, with grayish edgings to the feathers in the secondaries. However, in flight it comes into its own and shows a majestic outline, with the white underwing coverts forming white triangles and providing a distinctive identifying feature. The wings are held straight with the tips of the primaries bent upward and slightly forward as it slides effortlessly on its long broad wings. A short broad tail is flexed as it steers itself around the sky.

The California Condor has never been numerous, and one pair covers a huge territory. Its former range was along the United States' West Coast north to the Columbia river and south to Baja California and including Nevada, Mexico, and Texas. Its range has contracted and numbers have declined markedly since the beginning of the century, to the point where its domain was confined to a relatively small area of south coastal mountains of California, from where the few remaining birds have been taken into a controlled breeding program in order to save them from extinction. Though persecuted by man, recent evidence has shown their demise may well have been brought about by birds dying from lead poisoning after ingesting shot from the remains of hunter-killed mammals. Results from autopsies carried out on four birds in the early 1980s showed three had died form this cause. Shooting, other forms of poisoning, birds flying into power lines, and the like have all contributed to bringing this species to the edge of extinction.

This portrait of a Black Vulture shows the gray, featherless head (which is red in the Turkey Vulture) and a slender finely hooked bill. Black and Turkey Vultures often occur together where their ranges overlap.

The Griffon Vulture is a most impressive bird, particularly in flight. The wings are very long and broad, with widely spread primaries forming rounded ends. The tail is very short and square. It is found over most of Spain and also in the Balkans, Greece, Turkey, and eastward into Asia Minor.

A typical carrion feeder, the Griffon Vulture has decreased in some areas where human activities have reduced the opportunities for scavenging. The Griffon Vulture was recently reintroduced to the French Pyrenees, where it was formerly persecuted to its extinction as a breeding bird.

Two Black Vultures are shown perched in a tree at Sanibel Island, Florida, an area where these birds are commonly found. Like the Turkey Vulture, this bird frequently sits with wings partly open to warm itself in the sun.

GRIFFON VULTURE *GYPS COPROTHERES*

Perhaps most typical of the Old World Vultures is the Griffon Vulture. It has very long, broad wings, with widely spread primaries forming rounded ends; the tail is short, dark, and squared. Its body plumage is sandy brown and contrasts with the dark wing and tail feathers. The head and neck are unfeathered but are covered with a creamy white down. The bill is strongly hooked but shorter than those of other closely related vultures. There is a ruff of creamy white feathers at the base of the neck, and at times the head is almost completely withdrawn in it.

The Griffon Vulture wheels about the sky of its rocky, mountainous domain, frequently spreading out over the flat plains to find the carrion on which it feeds. Many will gather at a carcass. At other times it is gregarious, often forming communal roosts on precipitous cliffs of favored locations.

Griffon Vultures are to be found in southern Europe and, though they have decreased in recent times, are still quite common in Spain. They also occur in northeast Africa and the Arabian peninsula, and then eastward through Asia to Kashmir and the Altai region.

The Lammergeier, or Bearded Vulture, is so named for the "beard" of black feathers beneath the bill. A giant of a bird with a ten-foot wing span, it shows a distinctive wedge-shaped tail in flight. A bird of high mountainous country, it is an Old World Vulture restricted mainly to the Drakensburg Mountains, the Ethiopian Massif, the Atlas Mountains, the Pyrenees, the Alps, and the Himalayas.

The Egyptian Vulture is one of the smaller vultures. Its fine bill enables it to extract marrow from bones. This bird is also widely known for its so-called tool-using ability; that is, it picks up small rocks to hurl at Ostrich eggs in order to get at the yolk.

The King Vulture is an extraordinary-looking bird, displaying a bizarre combination of colors and skin folds set on a bare neck trimmed by a ruff of fine feathers. The rest of the plumage is basically black and white. A bird of tropical forests, it somehow manages to find carcasses invariably hidden from sight beneath the tree canopy.

25

WHITE-BACKED VULTURE *GYPS AFRICANUS*

This Old World Vulture is by far the most common Vulture in southern areas of Africa and is probably more numerous than all other species of African Vulture put together. A bird of savanna lands and open grassy plains, it is found from Eritrea, Sudan, and Senegal southward to all of southern Africa except the Cape. It is particularly abundant in the big game reserves, where there is a constant supply of carrion. The carcass of an antelope can quickly attract as many as two hundred White-backed Vultures, while one thousand birds might gather around a dead elephant.

The White-backed Vulture feeds by tearing at a carcass with its powerful beak. However, it cannot rip open an intact animal and must wait for another predator to give it a start. Like most other vultures, the feet are weak and the talons short and play no part in securing its prey.

The plumage of the White-backed Vulture is generally brownish with the primaries and tail blackish brown. The lower back is white, from which the bird gets its name, but this feature is not fully developed until it reaches an age of six or seven. The sexes are similar, as with other large vultures.

The White-backed Vulture spends much of its time perched rather than in flight. It usually goes to roost two to three hours before dark and probably flies for no more than eight hours in any day. There are rarely on the wing until the sun is well up, when there are sufficient hot air thermals on which they can soar without any great effort. The White-backed Vulture normally operates between five hundred to two thousand feet above ground and from this height can see many miles. In this way it locates its food, but also relies on other birds to lead it to a carcass. It has been reported that White-backed Vultures gorge themselves until they cannot fly, but this is rarely the case. After feeding they usually fly to the nearest tree, where they will stay for several hours digesting a meal.

White-backed Vultures always nest in trees, usually in small colonies. The nest is relatively small for such a large bird, but it is sufficiently solid to be used year after year. One egg is laid. Incubation lasts about forty-five days, possibly longer. The chick, which is covered in gray down, develops very slowly and is fed on a diet of regurgitated meat. After 120 to 130 days, the young bird can fly. The entire nesting cycle takes about six months.

The White-backed Vulture is the most common vulture in Southern Africa. It is not unusual for an antelope carcass in a game reserve to attract up to twenty birds, while a dead elephant could bring in one hundred feeding birds.

A White-backed Vulture surveys the scene from its lofty perch in the Kalahari National Park, South Africa. Vultures spend long hours just sitting around on the ground or in trees, if not disturbed, digesting their past meal.

Like other vultures, the White-backed Vulture soars to great heights seeking out prey with its incredible eyesight. This bird has located something and planes in on its huge expanse of wing; its downward-facing legs act as air brakes.

The White-backed Vulture feeds
by inserting its head and neck
into a carcass to gulp down
intestines and loose meat.
The large, conical bill—clearly
visible here—cannot tear skin.

Ruppell's Vulture is found in Senegal, Nigeria, and the Cameroons, eastward to Eritrea and Ethiopia and south through Uganda and Kenya to Tanganyika. This large vulture and the White-backed Vulture are usually the most numerous of the vultures to gather at a feeding opportunity, such as a buffalo kill after the lions have had their fill.

A Ruppell's Vulture shows its huge spread of wings, revealing the distinctive underwing pattern of creamy-edged dark feathers, which help to distinguish this bird from the similar White-backed Vulture.

RUPPELL'S VULTURE *GYPS RUEPPELLII*

Ruppell's Vulture superficially resembles the White-backed Vulture, but is slightly larger. It is a dark brown bird with a dark back. Feathering, especially on the underparts and wing coverts, is broadly edged with creamy white, giving it a scaly or spotted appearance. Immature birds appear very pale looking, as the pale feather margins are wider than in the adult.

It is found in the drier parts of Africa from Eritrea to the Sudan, south to parts of East Africa and West Africa.

Like the White-backed Vulture, it is a sociable species that roosts, feeds, and breeds in numbers. They tend more to roost on crags rather than trees and likewise prefer the same site for nesting. The nest itself is usually only a slight structure of sticks plastered with droppings, which at times can be scarcely seen under this whitewash. The clutch comprises one, and sometimes two, eggs and these tend to be laid in the dry season, though nesting can take place in all months of the year. The incubation and fledging period is equally as lengthy as that of the White-backed Vulture, and the young are in the nest for all of three months before they can fly.

With the exception of the White-backed Vulture it is usually the most numerous vulture at any carcass, where it forms a squabbling, seething mass. Within an hour or so there will be little left of even a large antelope or similar-sized carrion.

Ruppell's Vulture is basically a dark brown bird scaled by even rows of cream feather margins. This feature should quickly distinguish it from the slightly smaller White-backed Vulture, with which it is frequently found feeding at sources of carrion.

CRESTED CARACARA *POLYBORUS PLANCUS*

Though it belongs to the falcon family—which includes such dashing, agile fliers as the Peregrine, Hobby, and Merlin—the Crested Caracara is a comparatively slow-moving scavenging bird. There are actually nine species of Caracara of the subfamily Polyborinae, all of which have a more or less overall similar look, with longish legs and a powerful, eaglelike bill. They walk easily and quickly, spending a great deal of time on the ground feeding principally on carrion. Caracaras are found from the Central Americas and throughout South America.

The Crested Caracara is approximately Buzzard-sized but has long narrow wings, which give it a more slender outline. Blackish brown overall, it has a black cap, white throat and neck, and red-orange bare facial skin. Immature birds are browner, with the upperparts edged and spotted with buff, while the underparts are streaked. In flight, it shows white patches in its wing, which along with the white-banded tail are very conspicuous. It has a harsh, crackling call from which the bird gets its name.

Found through Central America and in southern California and Florida, where it frequents mainly open country, the species has many local names. In Mexico it is known as the Mexican Eagle, or Mexican Buzzard. In the United States, it is sometimes called the Common Caracara or Audubon's Caracara. In Argentina it is known as Comancho. The cackling call is usually uttered in the early morning or evening during the breeding season. The bird situates itself on a prominent perch and throws its head back until it almost touches the shoulders. Apart from these vociferous demonstrations, it is a fairly silent species.

The Crested Caracara builds a large, untidy nest of sticks usually lined with a variety of materials, such as skin, hair, bits of bone, and dried dung. Sometimes the same nest is used over several years. The site itself is quite variable and may be an isolated tree or giant cactus, while at times it could be under a rock overhang or simply on the ground.

The usual clutch is two to three pinkish white eggs, blotched with brown. Incubation is shared by both sexes for about twenty-eight days. The young remain in the nest for two months and feed on a variety of food. Though they are great scavengers, Crested Caracaras will take all manner of creatures, including birds, rats, rabbits, squirrels, skunks, snakes, young alligators, crabs, and fish. Caracaras flock together at locations where food supplies are easily obtained and sometimes join with vultures at carcasses.

The Common Caracara shows an eagle-like profile with its heavy, hooked bill; for which reason it is sometimes referred to as the Mexican Eagle. It is in fact Mexico's national bird. It is actually related to the falcons, even though its feeding behaviour is basically that of a scavenger.

Of the nine species of Caracara occurring from the Central Americas and southward in South America, Striated Caracara is confined to the Falkland Islands. A large black bird, it has white streaks on the neck and breast. There is a white band across the tail and a bright yellow facial skin crop and legs. It has made attacks on the introduced sheep on the islands; for this, not surprisingly, it has been persecuted.

With a wing span of about ten feet, the Lappet-faced Vulture is a most powerful and aggressive bird. It easily dominates and intimidates smaller vultures at any carcass and uses both feet and its massive bill to keep them away from a food source until it has had its fill.

This dramatic shot shows a Lappet-faced Vulture—or Nubian Vulture, as it is sometimes called—leaving its perch on a dead tree in the Masai Mara, Kenya.

2.
EAGLES THAT FEED ON FISH

OSPREY *PANDION HALIAETUS*

The Osprey, or Fish Hawk, as it is often called in North America, breeds in many parts of the world and globally is quite common. It is found widely in North America, northern and eastern Europe and some Mediterranean countries. It also nests in large parts of Asia, eastward to the Pacific Ocean, also occurring sporadically in Africa and around most of the coast of Australia.

As is usually the case with a species breeding in all continents, a number of different races have evolved. None of these, however, exhibit any great variance in appearance from the nominate race, *Pandion haliaetus*, which breeds throughout a major part of its overall range. This encompasses Europe, Africa, and across Asia. Apart from the

An Osprey roosts in an Australian pine tree at Big Pine Key, Florida, an area that supports a large number of nesting pairs of these fine birds, due in part to its many fishing opportunities.

In dramatic plunging dives or by snatching fish from the water's surface, the Osprey obtains its main source of food. Here a bird has taken a fish almost too big for it to carry away.

Atlantic Islands, Britain is at the western extremity of its Palearctic distribution. It is here that it has come back from extinction as a breeding bird to an established and flourishing breeding population, thanks to round-the-clock protection by the Royal Society for the Protection of Birds.

Resembling a medium-sized eagle, the Osprey is unique. A sole member of the family Pandionidae, it is almost exclusively a fish eater and has justly earned itself the other name of "Fish Hawk." The Osprey cruises along on powerful wings, haunting mountain lakes to coastal marshes, rivers, and estuaries, wherever such habitat occurs within its range. From forty to one hundred feet above the surface, it scans the water for signs of a fish. When a ripple of water or the flash of scales is seen, it plunges with wings half folded (sometimes momentarily hovering beforehand), entering the water feet first, sending up a cloud of spray. The power of the plunge dive is such that the Osprey is almost completely submerged, with often only the wing tips showing above the water. The uniquely adapted talons are all of equal length, with the outer one reversible (as an owl), giving the bird a secure grip of its slippery prey. The surface of the feet are also covered with spines, which further aid its grip. Once in flight the fish is adjusted to a head-forward position to reduce drag. The fish might weigh one or two pounds, which could be one- or two-thirds of the bird's weight! The catch is normally carried to a nearby perch to be eaten at its leisure, if not to feed to a hungry family. If fish are scarce, it will take frogs and at times small birds.

The nest is a bulky structure of sticks invariably near water and sometimes over it. The nest sites are often traditional, and favorite trees are used over many years. The nest is added to annually and at times collapses under its own weight.

The clutch is usually two to four eggs, young hatching after about thirty-two to thirty-eight days. Fledging takes another thirty-two days, after which time the young can feed themselves.

The Osprey about to land on a tree displays its white underbody and strongly marked wings with dark patches. This female shows its necklace of dark streaking on the upper breast.

In the United States, it is colonial where large numbers nest in close proximity to each other, especially along the East Coast. At the turn of the century there was a huge colony of over three hundred on Gardines Island off Long Island, New York.

Highly migratory European birds move to Africa, frequently stopping off to feed, wherever suitable conditions are located en route. The species ceased to breed in Scotland at the turn of the century, brought to extinction by shooting and the taking of eggs. In the more recent enlightened times, visiting Ospreys to Scotland have been protected and encouraged to nest. In 1958 a pair nested at Loch Garten. This locale has been wardened and watched over by the RSPB ever since, and the number of Ospreys nesting has increased each year. Special viewing arrangements have provided thousands of visitors to the area an opportunity to observe these exciting birds at their nest.

A male Osprey perched atop a tree is thrown into stark relief against a dark background. The white head and prominent eyestripe are most noticeable here.

A pair of Ospreys mates on their island home, Sanibel, Florida. Their bulky nest nearby has already been completed and is ready to receive its clutch of usually three eggs.

The Palm Nut Vulture is really misnamed, as its feeding habits are not those typical of vultures at all. It is almost exclusively vegetarian, feeding mainly on the fruits of the oil palm. It does, however, sometimes eat carrion and occasionally catches fish. The species is found in West Africa eastward across the middle of the continent to the east coast.

BALD EAGLE *HALIALEETUS LEUCOCEPHALUS*

Declared the national emblem of the United States of America in 1782, the Bald Eagle was, however, not everybody's first choice for this honor. Its scavenging habits and rather timid disposition did not endear it all. However, with its distinctive brown-and-white plumage, the Bald Eagle is a striking-looking bird with a fierce, powerful expression, justifying its selection in the eyes of most Americans. The United States is, of course, not alone in choosing an eagle as its emblem for their are many countries that have eagles as their emblem, as a means of reflecting the power, strength, and mobility these birds embody. Though there are many bird of prey species in North America, the continent is home to only two species of eagle, the other being the Golden Eagle, whereas in Europe there are eight species of nesting eagles.

A pair of Bald Eagles at their nest site on Marco Island, Florida. Many such sites are traditional and are used over many years, the nest being added to annually, often reaching huge proportions before being destroyed by winter gales.

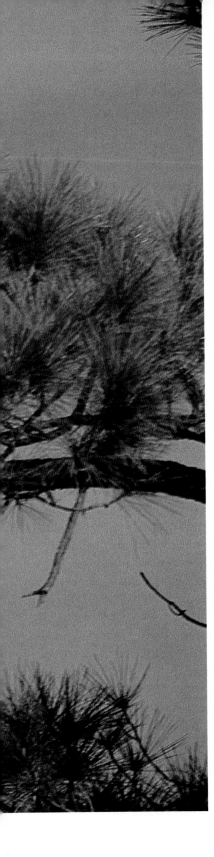

Carrying a fish in its talons, an adult American Bald Eagle returns to its nest near Naples in Florida, an area where the species is still quite commonly found.

As a breeding bird, the Bald Eagle is confined to most of the North American continent ranging from Alaska in the north through Canada and then as far south as Florida in the east and southern California in the west.

Despite its heraldic importance the Bald Eagle has not always been treated as well as perhaps a national emblem should be, for in the past it has been persecuted by the fish and fur industries, with bounties paid for dead Bald Eagles. Up until 1963 they were still shot; from the 1920s through the 1960s, about one hundred thousand had been slaughtered.

In relatively recent times—particularly since the end of World War II—breeding success of the species has been seriously affected by pesticides and pollution. Along with loss of habitat, these factors have all combined to greatly reduce the total breeding population. In the East it has been reduced to two major areas: the North Chesapeake Bay and Florida, with the coastal states in between holding but few pairs. However, the Bald Eagle is now protected throughout the land by the National Emblem Law, and this should ensure an improvement in its future status.

Bald Eagles nest in trees from seventy to up to one hundred feet high or on cliff faces often in totally inaccessible places. The nest is a bulky structure of sticks. The usual clutch is two eggs. Both parents take turn to incubate for around thirty-five days. The young stay in the nest for between seventy-two and seventy-four days.

Fish is a major part of the diet of Bald Eagles, however, these are mainly taken when dead or dying. They will also steal fish from Ospreys. In winter, birds and small mammals are more frequently taken. Though not as common as in the past, impressive gatherings can still be seen in British Columbia and Alaska. There Bald Eagles come together to feed on the schools of salmon and herring swimming up the rivers to spawn. At such times between three thousand and four thousand have been counted in November on the Chilkat River in Alaska, where they feed on the dead and dying salmon.

A pair of adult Bald Eagles are pictured against the intense blue of an Everglades sky. Such characteristics as a plumage pattern of white head and tail, dark body, and huge yellow bill make them readily identifiable.

Two Bald Eagles roost in hoar-frosted trees in the Chilkat River area, where thousands of these birds gather in early winter to feed on the dead and dying salmon that come to spawn there.

A lone Bald Eagle, perched along the Chilkat River, is just one of the several thousand that gather there in the winter to feed at the spawning runs of salmon.

A Bald Eagle glides toward its nest site trailing some grasses snatched from the ground by its powerful talons. These will serve as a lining to its otherwise totally stick-and-branch-constructed nest.

Quite vociferous at times, the harsh "kark, kark" calls of the Bald Eagle can be frequently heard, particularly during the breeding season. At such times the constant contact between each bird forms an essential part of their pair bonding behavior.

An impressive portrait of America's national emblem, the Bald Eagle, conveys the power and strength of this fine bird of prey.

The adult White-tailed Eagle has an all-white tail, which along with its massive build and wide span of its very broad wings, should make identification of the bird in flight fairly easy. However, immature Golden Eagles do have a lot of white in their tail and could be mistaken for the larger White-tailed Eagle.

The far-reaching call of the African Fish Eagle is one of the characteristic background sounds of the African countryside. Widely distributed and common throughout most of its range, it is to be found in the vicinity of lakes, swamps, rivers, and flooded areas, where it feeds mainly on fish snatched from the surface with its feet. It also takes large rodents and at times various water birds.

3. AGILE-FLYING FOREST HUNTERS

NORTHERN GOSHAWK *ACCIPITER GENTILIS*

The largest and fiercest of the accipiters—short-winged long-tailed hawks—the Northern Goshawk is approximately Buzzard-sized. As with most of the Accipiters, the female is the larger of the sexes.

In general appearance it resembles an oversize Common Sparrowhawk (*Accipiter nisus*), but it should always be remembered that some female Sparrowhawks can be quite large. When seen from below, the bird's densely gray-barred underparts and conspicuously white undertail coverts are visible. The wings appear broader based than those of the Sparrowhawk and when not soaring look more pointed. The upperparts are a dark slaty gray, and there is a noticeable white eyestripe. Mature birds have a red eye. Both sexes are similar, except for disparity in size. The immature bird is brown above with buffish underparts,

Much larger than the similar Sparrowhawk, the Northern Goshawk can weave its way through quite dense woodland to seize its prey in full flight. The long tail and broad wings, which allow this precision flying, are clearly seen in this photograph.

The name Goshawk is a corruption of "goose-hawk," for this bird is capable of taking birds that size. One of the "accipiters," or broad-winged hawks of the northern European and North American forests, it is quite common throughout most of its range. Here a female Goshawk mantles her prey, in this instance a Hooded Merganser.

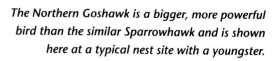

boldly marked with dark brown streaking, heaviest on the flanks, and the long tail is brown marked with dark wavy bands. The tip of the tail is edged with white.

Mainly resident throughout its range, it is widely distributed throughout the holarctic region from within the Arctic Circle to the Mediterranean, central Asia, and southern Japan. It is to be found virtually everywhere throughout the forested areas of Europe and is quite common in those parts where human activity is least, for the Goshawk is probably one of the most attacked raptors there is in Europe. It was, in fact, almost exterminated as a breeding bird in Britain, but is now making a comeback. The current breeding stock in some areas, ironically emanating from escaped falconer birds, is identified as such by their "jesses."

The Goshawk is typically a bird of forests and wooded districts in both lowland and mountainous regions, favoring coniferous woodland particularly. It is virtually absent from the North American deciduous woodland.

In direct flight it is much like the Sparrowhawk flying very fast, accelerating rapidly as required to overtake its prey. The powerful wings and long tail enable it to thread its way through trees with remarkable agility, matching every twist and turn of any bird that it pursues. The victim is caught with the feet, and small birds are invariably killed instantly by the powerful gripping talons. These are usually taken to a favorite plucking post, often a tree stump, where the feathers are removed. Such locations can be easily identified by the many feathers scattered around. Birds of varying sizes are taken, from quite small species, such as finches, up to the size of wood pigeons and crows; even Capercaillie are captured. Mammals also feature in the Goshawk's diet, and squirrels, chipmunk, rats, mice, and the like are all readily taken.

The Northern Goshawk not only preys on all manner of bird species but also takes mammals and squirrels. This photograph shows an immature bird that has just caught a gray squirrel.

Keeping to deep woodland, the Goshawk is not always easily observed and does not take to the open skies as frequently as the "buteo" hawks. However, in the spring it indulges in spectacular display flights above the chosen territory, soaring and diving from great heights. The usually rather bulky nest is built by the female close to the trunk of a tall, mature tree. Supported by a branch, it can be as low as fifteen feet to upward of seventy feet. Fresh green foliage is often added in the same way as the buzzard decorates its nest.

Clutch size ranges from two to six eggs, which are whitish and usually unmarked, but soon become stained. Incubation is carried out entirely by the female and lasts for five weeks. The young fledge after about six weeks.

Goshawks are not known for any major migratory movements, but there is a general dispersal southward from their northernmost breeding areas. Where prey is available throughout the winter, distances traveled from the natal home are quite small. In mid-Europe, for example, ringing recoveries have shown this to be no more than twenty-five to thirty miles.

Though both male and female Sparrowhawk share in nest building, the female alone incubates the eggs and broods and cares for the chicks. In this picture it is the larger female that carefully feeds the youngsters with morsels of food torn from prey mainly brought by the male.

The usual Sparrowhawk nest is a flat, untidy, loosely built platform of locally available twigs. The old nest of a crow or pigeon is often used as a foundation. The normal clutch is five to six eggs, which are bluish white to whitish or pale greenish, sometimes unmarked but generally blotched, spotted, and streaked chocolate brown.

SPARROWHAWK *ACCIPITER NISUS*

Perhaps the most familiar "hawk" to British birdwatchers—by name anyway—is the Sparrowhawk. Quite frequently, however, the Kestrel (which is a falcon) is misidentified or mistakenly called a Sparrowhawk. However they are really quite easily distinguished, as their modes of hunting are quite different.

When hunting the Sparrowhawk flies fast and low, with three or four beats of its rounded wings followed by a long glide. Moving along hedgerows, the borders of woods, woodland rides, and watercourses it surprises small birds, which it captures with its talons, thrusting out its long yellow legs to do so. It also shows incredible flying skill as it threads through a wood or copse to pursue any prey that escapes the first pass. It will also chase and outfly birds in the open. The female has dark brownish upperparts, with a white stripe above and behind the eye, and whitish underparts finely barred with dark brown. The much smaller male has a slaty blue-gray back and underparts finely barred with reddish brown. During their nuptial flight, a pair will soar at considerable heights over the breeding territory. The Sparrowhawk has a variety of calls in the breeding season, the usual alarm note near the nest being a rapid, harsh "kek-kek-kek-kek."

The nest is a flat, untidy platform of twigs. Commonly in a conifer, it is usually close to the main trunk twenty or more feet above the ground, the old nest of Crow or Pigeon often used to form the base. The five to six eggs are bluish white or pale green, blotched or streaked with chocolate brown, or sometimes unmarked; they are laid in May and there is one brood.

The bird is widely distributed throughout Europe, extending westward from Britain and Ireland, eastward to Japan, and north to south from beyond the tree line to north Africa. It is notably absent from North America, where the equivalent ecological niche there is filled by the Sharp-shinned Hawk (*Accipiter striatus*).

The Sparrowhawk hunts with a rapid, dashing flight, often surprising small birds along woodland rides or forest edges. This picture shows a falconer's bird that has captured a Robin (Erithacus rubecula).

Cooper's Hawk is very similar to the Sharp-shinned Hawk but has a longer, more rounded tail and a large head, with the adult male showing a dark capped appearance. It is uncommon throughout North America and probably declining. Cooper's Hawk generally inhabits broken deciduous woodlands and often perches on telegraph poles, a habit it does not share with the Sharp-shinned Hawk.

The Sharp-shinned Hawk is distinguished from the similar Cooper's Hawk by a shorter, squared tail—which often appears notched when folded—and by a relatively smaller head and neck. The Cooper's Hawk is also much darker on the crown. Common over most of the United States, it can be found in mixed woodland, where it preys chiefly on small birds. The bird shown here is an immature.

BROWN GOSHAWK *ACCIPITER FASCIATUS*

The Brown Goshawk or Australian Goshawk is a typical large accipiter displaying a fierce appearance and having rounded wings, a long, square tail, and powerful legs and talons for catching its prey.

In many ways it fills the same ecological niche as its counterpart in the Northern Hemisphere, the Northern Goshawk (*Accipiter gentilis*). It is, however, a somewhat smaller bird and quite different in coloration and markings. It bears a strong resemblance to another Australian accipiter, the Collared Sparrowhawk (*A. cirrhocephalus*). Both these birds have blue-gray or dark brown upperparts, a rufous half collar, and underparts heavily barred with rufous. In both species the males are smaller than the females. However, the female Brown Goshawk is very much larger and heavier looking than the male Collared Sparrowhawk, but a large female Collared Sparrowhawk is much the same size as a small male Brown Goshawk; as a consequence the two species can be easily confused.

The Brown Goshawk is found throughout the whole of Australia, apart from, perhaps, the very dry central regions. It also occurs in Tasmania, New Guinea, Reynell Island, and other islands north and west as far as Flores, Timor, and Christmas Island. Resident throughout this range, it favors wooded areas with forest clearings and more open areas with scattered trees. It seems to avoid the densest forest regions altogether.

It is equally as secretive as the Northern Goshawk and it is often overlooked, though in suitable habitat it is quite common. Again as with the Northern Goshawk, it adopts two modes of hunting, capturing its prey either by pouncing on it from a perch or by surprising it during flight. In the open it has a characteristic gliding flight interspersed with short series of flaps. Mammals form a major part of the diet, but it takes a wide range of bird species, from parrots downward in size. It also takes rats, snakes, lizards, and insects. The nest is like that of other accipiters, quite a bulky affair of sticks, frequently using the foundation of a previous nest of its own or that of some other species. The nest is usually placed near the top of a tall tree, and in Australia a eucalyptus is often favored.

Two to four eggs are laid; these are bluish white occasionally streaked red-brown. Incubation and fledging periods are similar to other accipiters, and as is generally the case the female does most of the caring of the young.

The Brown Goshawk, or Australian Goshawk as it is also known is to be found throughout most of Australia except the very driest interior. This photograph shows an immature bird, a very brown looking bird, from which the bird gets its name. The adults however are much more colourful.

4.
LOW-FLYING STRIKERS

RED KITE *MILVUS MILVUS*

The Red Kite is readily identified by its long, reddish, deeply forked tail and its long, narrow, sharply angled wings, which show contrasting white patches on the underside. The main body plumage is brown above and paler below, while the head is grayish white. Its flight is buoyant and graceful with long glides and slow wing beats. The long tail is used as a rudder, which is constantly twisted and fanned as it maneuvers elegantly about the sky seeking out its prey—which can be any carrion it comes across.

Small mammals and birds are also taken and very un-"bird-of-prey"-like it will, at times, feed avidly on worms.

A Red Kite shows its deeply forked chestnut tail and narrow, strongly angled wings as it quarters an open grassy area seeking out its prey. This could be some small mammal, large insect, or even an earthworm. However, it will also readily take carrion.

In Britain the Red Kite has a small but growing population thanks to intensive protection. Virtually extinct in the early part of this century, the bird has made a comeback in mid-Wales, where there are now fifty to sixty pairs.

In Britain this bird is widely known as an example of successful bird protection, having been saved from almost total extinction as a breeding species—an amazing reversal of its earlier status! At the beginning of this century only a handful were left, after having been a common widespread bird of prey. In the fifteenth and sixteenth centuries, they were a protected species serving a useful purpose in clearing London streets of refuse. However, by the eighteenth century, they were no longer essential scavengers and became less tolerated as more and more preyed on backyard chickens. Over the ensuing century, they dramatically declined in numbers, no doubt due to the lack of carrion and the growing importance of game shooting, with all birds of prey considered to be a potential danger to pheasant and partridge rearing.

During this period, and even into the twentieth century, many different species of birds of prey suffered, with relatively slow flying and obvious targets, such as Red Kites, suffering in particular. During the period 1830 to 1850, the Red Kite disappeared from most English counties, and by 1870 the last pair had gone. Ten years later the last Scottish breeding pair was recorded in Perthshire. However a small number managed to survive in mid-Wales.

From small beginnings a Welsh Kite Protection Society developed and with the aid of the RSPB helped to increase the population from no more than half a dozen pairs in the 1940s to in excess of sixty pairs up to the present time. Though still relatively common in parts of Europe, it has suffered a decline throughout its range over the past three hundred to four hundred years for the same reasons that led to the decline of the British population.

The Red Kite breeds in Sweden and the Baltic States south to Spain, the west Mediterranean islands, Italy, the northern Balkan, and western Russia. It also extends eastward through Asia Minor to northern Iran, and southward to northwest Africa and to the Canary Isles. The Welsh population seem to be mainly sedentary, but those in northern and central Europe migrate southward, some reaching north Africa.

The sharply defined black and white plumage pattern and deeply forked tail of the American Swallow-tailed Kite make identification easy. In agile and graceful flight, it takes flying insects, but it also swoops down on snakes, lizards, and young birds.

The Pale Chanting Goshawk is very similar to the Dark Chanting Goshawk but prefers more open country. As its name suggests, it is a much lighter bird than the aforementioned species. A low-flying striker, it will often perch motionlessly while awaiting the appearance of prey.

A highly migratory species, the Pallid Harrier nests mainly eastward through much of the Soviet Union. In winter birds move to Africa or the Indian subcontinent. This photograph shows an immature bird on migration through the Middle East, where it has just captured another migrant bird of prey, a Hobby (Falco subbuteo).

BLACK-SHOULDERED KITE
ELANUS CAERULEUS

Formerly called the Black-winged Kite, this bird is probably one of the most beautiful of all birds of prey. It is predominantly white with a soft blue-gray back and wings with black shoulders. The white tail is forked. The primaries are gray above and black below, giving it a striking black-and-white appearance when seen in flight. At close range the red eyes enhance its overall stunning appearance.

This bird breeds throughout a large part of Africa, except the northern deserts, through to India down to Malaysia, Indonesia, and Australia. In North America it is limited to California and parts of Central America and then discontinuously in South America. In southern Europe it breeds in Portugal but is a rare visitor elsewhere in Europe. A bird of open country, it frequents all savanna-type situations to open semidesert, from sea level up to an elevation of nine thousand feet. Its hunting mode is to quarter an area flying fifty to two hundred feet above the ground, frequently hovering like a Kestrel. Its characteristic kill method is a graceful coup de grace, dropping seemingly gently into the grass. The wings are held high above the back, the angle controlling the descent. In this way it seizes small animals and at times, birds, as well as large insects. Sometimes insects are caught in the air.

Basically a sedentary bird, there is little or no large migratory movement by this species, but northern populations tend to wander farther afield in winter. A pair stays together for much of the year and can usually be found in close proximity to each other.

At the beginning of the breeding season birds soar high above the chosen nesting area, but no really spectacular display behaviors have been observed. The nest is normally in a tree, but where there are no trees a rocky ledge is used. Both birds help to build the nest, which is a slight structure of twigs, flat and loosely put together.

Three to four eggs are laid, which are a handsome creamy color that is streaked, blotched, and smeared with dark brown or purplish markings. In temperate regions the eggs are laid in the spring, while in tropical areas, the dry season is the main nesting period.

The female mostly incubates and is fed at the nest by the male for this twenty-six day period. Thirty to thirty-five days later the young are sufficiently developed to leave the nest, but return to it at intervals after their first flight. For a time they continue to be fed by the parents.

The Black Kite is a successful scavenger found throughout many parts of the world. It favors open woodlands, forests, and open desert-type habitats, where it feeds on carrion.

A female Hen Harrier is pictured at its nest in the bracken of a western Scottish island, stronghold of the British breeding population. Note the owl-like expression and the heavily barred tail. The distinctive white rump very evident in flight is in this instance hidden by the folded wings.

HEN HARRIER, NORTHERN HARRIER *CIRCUS CYANEUS*

This species has the widest distribution of that group of birds of prey known as harriers. There are ten species of harrier in the world, all of which are generally long-legged, long-winged and quite long in the body. They have a characteristic easy, bouyant flight low over the ground, hold their wings in a V, and occasionally hover. In this manner they quarter a chosen area searching for small mammals. Harriers have unusually large ear openings hidden by a ruff of facial feathers, which give them a distinctly owlish appearance.

The Hen Harrier occurs across Europe and Asia while the very similar Northern Harrier is to be found only in North America.

In Britain and Europe the Hen Harrier occurs in a great variety of habitats, including moors, coastal and inland marshes, dunes, and open grassy areas. In North America the Northern Harrier seems to favor marshes moreso than its European counterpart. In winter most of the American birds move to coastal and river marshes. In North America, breeding range extends from Alaska to Labrador and Newfoundland south to California, Arizona, New Mexico, Texas, the central states, and Virginia.

In Eurasia the Hen Harrier may be found breeding from the tundra south to western Europe, and eastward across Asia to northern China. Both male and female are quite dramatic in their own ways. The male is a beautiful, soft pearl gray all over with dark wing tips and dark trailing edge to the wing. The rump is white. At a distance it looks so pale that at long range it could easily be mistaken for a gull. The male American subspecies has small rufous spots on its white underparts.

The female has dark brown upperparts, while the underparts are buff or pale brown and heavily streaked with darker brown. The long tail is barred and the rump white.

On dry ground the nest is a shallow cup lined with fine grasses, while in wetter areas it is a platform of reeds or sedges. The four to six eggs are bluish white, sometimes with spots and streaks of reddish brown. Incubation varies from twenty-nine to thirty-five days. After another thirty to thirty-five days, the young are fully feathered.

The Hen Harrier is normally a silent bird, but at the nest it has a rapidly repeated chattering "ka-ke-ke-ke" call when excited or alarmed. In Britain it is a Schedule I bird and afforded special protection. Breeding mainly in the Orkneys, Outer Hebrides, and Ireland, it has in recent years established itself on the Scottish mainland and is spreading to northern England and Wales.

The Hen Harrier, as with other harriers, hunts in a very distinctive way, quartering the ground at low level with gliding, buoyant flight wings held in a shallow V; it momentarily stalls or hovers briefly before plunging down to snatch its prey, which might be some small mammal, amphibian, lizard, or bird.

A female Hen Harrier is pictured
at its nest site, which contains
one young bird. Considering
the normal clutch size is four to
six eggs, this is not a very good
hatching success rate.

A female Hen Harrier, almost hidden by a beakful of nesting material, displays an intent to line the nest scrape with plenty of grasses.

Note the disparity of sizes in this nest of young Hen Harriers due to asynchronous hatching. Incubation usually begins with the laying of the second egg, but sometimes with the first, which accounts for their different ages. The smallest of the chicks will probably not survive.

In some species of birds, the male and female are quite different in plumage coloration. Here, a pair of Marsh Harriers—at their nest site, typically located in a reed bed—displays such sexual dimorphism.

The Snail Kite is a marshland-haunting species found from Florida and eastern Mexico to the pampas of Argentina and Uruguay, as well as Cuba and the Isle of Pines. Its diet is largely comprised of freshwater snails caught with its feet and extracted with its elongated, thin upper mandible. In the United States it was formerly called the Everglade Kite, as it was once more common and widespread in this region than it is today.

A local resident throughout most of the Ethiopian region, the Harrier Hawk is but sparsely distributed in Central Africa, where it is also called Gymmogene, or "bare cheek." This feature of an otherwise basically gray-and-black-looking hawk is most interesting, as the featherless area of skin changes color from yellow to red when the bird becomes excited. Apparently it also changes from yellow in the early part of the day to red by the afternoon as the temperature increases.

5.
SKY HUNTERS
OF THE PLAINS
AND GRASSLANDS

EURASIAN BUZZARD *BUTEO BUTEO*

The Eurasian Buzzard is perhaps one of the most familiar of the "buteo" hawks in Britain, Europe, and Russia through to China and Japan. In Britain it is sometimes referred to as the "Tourist Eagle" or "Poorman's Eagle," for this bird is more frequently seen in Scotland than the Golden Eagle, which visitors there hope to catch a glimpse of, but which is not so common or widespread.

Though quite a bit smaller than the Golden Eagle, with only a four-

In direct flight, especially when flushed from a sitting position, the Eurasian Buzzard is slow and ponderous, the rather labored wing beats belying its agility. But when hunting it launches itself from a tree or post and sweep downward in gliding flight to seize its hapless prey, which is often a rabbit.

The Eurasian Buzzard's main prey comprises small mammals, especially rabbits. Voles and moles are also caught, while carrion is readily taken. Birds are occasionally captured by surprise and these range in size from crows, partridges, grouses, and moorhens, to Skylarks, Meadow Pipits, and Great Tits. Snakes, frogs, toads, lizards, and large insects are also included in a varied diet.

foot wing span, it does however demonstrate eaglelike qualities as it spirals in wide circles on its broad, motionless wings, with primaries spread like the fingers of a hand. At such times its far-reaching "mewing" call may drift downward from on high. Some birds will circle for hours on motionless wings seeking out hot air thermals, which will help to keep them aloft without expending too much energy wing flapping. Buzzards favor hilly countryside with wooded valleys and escarpments, but are equally at home in more well-wooded lowland country in some parts of their range.

The plumage varies greatly among individuals, but generally appears dark brown mottled with white below. Some, however, are very pale with the occasional almost totally white bird. The eyes are yellow, as is the cere and the legs in all cases. This can vary in intensity, depending on the type of diet. The female Buzzard is invariably much larger than the male, and when together the difference in size is readily noted.

The nest can be on a cliff ledge or in a tree and comprises a substantial structure of sticks and small branches lined with a variety of vegetable material. The pair frequently decorate the nest with sprays of greenery from either conifers of broad-leaved trees as available. Two or three eggs is the usual clutch. The eggs are dull white blotched and smeared with reddish or chocolate brown. Incubation is by both parents and takes around thirty-three to thirty-five days. Fledging takes between forty to forty-five days, sometimes a little longer.

The male brings food to the female, who tears it into suitable morsels to feed to the newly hatched young for the first few days. As they grow they are then able to feed themselves.

The Buzzard is a great opportunist and will feed on a whole range of prey, favoring small mammals mice, rats, voles—while birds, lizards, snakes, frogs, even earthworms, and beetles are not overlooked. It will also feed on carrion as available. It has been claimed that Buzzards take game chicks and farmyard poultry, which may be true on rare occasions, but this omnivorous bird of prey can never be considered a threat to man's husbandry.

A well-developed Buzzard chick about four weeks old, this individual still retains vestiges of its downy feathering. It will be a further two weeks before it is fully fledged and is capable of flight.

Adults are very variable and can be very dark or very pale. Generally they are dark brown, mottled with white below. When perched they do not look that impressive, but in flight they soar majestically on broad, motionless wings often for hours on end.

Confined to the Galapagos, the Galapagos Hawk was once a common species throughout these islands. The shooting of this bird and predation by feral cats has greatly reduced its numbers. About 150 pairs remain. These are now protected, and it is hoped that this threatened species can at least maintain its status, if not improve upon it.

The Eurasian Buzzard's usual clutch is two eggs; three are frequently laid, occasionally four, and rarely five or six. Very old birds may only lay one egg. White in color, sometimes with a bluish tinge, they are usually blotched or spotted sometimes quite heavily covered with dark brown markings. They may also be marked sparingly, as in this instance.

The most common "buteo" in the United States, the adult Red-tailed Hawk has a reddish upper tail and a paler red undertail. The general plumage is extremely variable, with both light and dark phases. On the Great Plains, a pale version known as Krider's Hawk is found, while in Alaska and Canada a very dark-plumaged form called Harlan's Hawk occurs. This was formerly considered to be a separate species.

A bird of many different types of habitat, the Red-tailed Hawk is equally at home in woods, but also more open areas, such as plains, prairie land, and deserts. Here a Red-tailed Hawk feeds its young in a typical tree nest site.

RED-TAILED HAWK *BUTEO JAMACIENSIS*

North America is well populated with "buteo," or broad-winged, hawks. Of the ten or so species occurring, the Red-tailed Hawk is the commonest and most widespread. Found from the frozen wastes of Alaska and the Yukon to southerly desert, it inhabits woodland and open spaces, plains, prairies, and prairie groves.

The Red-tailed Hawk takes its name from the adult bird's major plumage feature, a bright red tail; however, in the immature bird this is grayish brown lined with blackish bars. The plumage of the Red-tailed Hawk is extremely variable. In the East especially, most "Redtails" show a belly band of dark streaks on whitish underparts, with a dark bar on the leading edge of the underwing contrasting with paler wing linings. The red uppertail is paler on the underside; variable pale mottling on the scapulars contrasts with the dark mantle, often forming a noticeable V shape on perched birds. Many southwestern Redtails lack the dark, streaky belly band of the eastern birds and display uniformly light underparts; the tail in this color phase is dark reddish on the upperside.

The so-called Harlan's Hawk was formerly considered to be a separate species. It does look quite different with its overall dark plumage, a dusky white tail, a diffuse blackish terminal band and showing some white streaking in the breast. This form breeds in Alaska and Canada. After nesting is complete these birds move south to winter in the central United States.

The Great Plains version of the Red-tailed Hawk is the so-called Krider's Hawk, which has paler underparts and a whitish tail with a pale reddish hue, while in flight it shows pale rectangular patches at the base of the primaries on the upperwing.

Like other "buteo" hawks, Redtails spiral across the sky using updraughts and thermals to keep them aloft without too much wing flapping as search for prey. Although Redtails spend long hours in flight, they also indulge in "wait-and-see" hunting. Using a favorite perch, the bird watches over its selected area on the lookout for any unsuspecting prey. Small rodents, mainly mice, form a major part of the bird's diet, but birds, snakes, and insects are also taken whenever the opportunity arises.

Dependent upon the type of habitat they're in, Redtails build nests either in conifers or broadleaved trees, or on the ledge of a suitable rock face. A sizable nest of sticks is constructed each year, though sometimes one from a previous year may be refurbished.

The usual clutch is two to five eggs: these are white blotched with reddish brown. The young hatch after four to five weeks and leave the nest to hunt with their parents after a further five to six weeks.

Against a snow-covered backdrop, a Red-tailed Hawk sweeps the area as it seeks its prey, which are mainly small rodents.

73

Found in dry open country, the Ferruginous Hawk frequently perches on trees and poles or on the ground. A fairly common species throughout its range in the middle and eastern United States, it is thought to be declining in numbers. This bird often hovers while hunting.

Also known as the Jackal Buzzard, the Augur Buzzard is probably East Africa's most frequently sighted bird of prey— perhaps perched on a telegraph pole or acacia tree. It feeds mainly on rats, mice, and small reptiles.

There are three different races of the Augur Buzzard in Africa. This is the race Buteo r. augur, which has mainly white underparts, as clearly shown in this photograph.

A mainly sedentary bird of open steppe or rocky country, the Long-legged Buzzard's plumage coloration is generally much paler than its counterparts to the north. Most easily confused with the Steppe Buzzard and occasionally the Rough-legged Buzzard, it is a very inactive species, often sitting for long hours on a chosen perch.

The Red-shouldered Hawk is a fairly common bird of the mixed woodlands of eastern America. The red shoulders and white wing markings help to identify the species, with the reddish wing linings of the underparts most noticeable in flight. There is a "Florida" form, which is smaller and paler, while the Californian western population is much more colorful on the underparts, though the red shoulders are less distinct.

A Red-shouldered Hawk sits upright on its perch, where it may stay for a long period, typical behavior of many birds of prey. This photograph shows the paler Florida form of the bird.

A Red-shouldered Hawk displays its distinctive underwing patterns as it wrestles with its prey, a snake taken in its Everglades domain.

RED-SHOULDERED HAWK *BUTEO LINEATUS*

A fairly common "buteo" hawk of moist, mixed woodlands in the eastern United States, the red-shouldered hawk is also found along parts of the West Coast zone from Oregon to Mexico. A little smaller than a European Buzzard, the Red-shouldered Hawk is so named for the rich, reddish brown patches on its shoulders. A relatively long-winged and long-tailed bird, its flight is, however, accipiterlike, with several quick wing beats followed by a glide. From underneath the red-dish wing linings and underparts, narrow white bands on a dark tail and white patches on the base of the primaries help to identify this bird. The red shoulders are, actually, not a very good field mark, and in the case of the darker western form they are even harder to detect. There is also a very pale form of this bird found in the extreme south of Florida.

In many parts of the northeastern United States, the Red-shouldered Hawk is the commonest hawk, with a breeding density of probably one pair every square mile, in favorable areas. Prenesting display consists of high, soaring flight accompanied by a great deal of screaming calls. These take place quite early in the year and form a familiar welcome sign of the approaching spring.

The favored nest site is in a tree, rarely less than thirty feet above the ground and is often placed twice this height. It is invariably sited in the main fork of a deciduous tree or if in conifer then close to the main trunk.

More northerly nesting birds lay three to four eggs, while those in Florida tend to produce smaller clutches. The eggs are white and heavily blotched with dark markings. Incubation is often shared by both of the sexes and lasts for around twenty-eight days; the fledging period lasts for the same amount of time.

Red-shouldered Hawks spend long periods perched on vantage points, such as a telegraph pole or dead tree, on the lookout for any suitable prey. This comprises a wide range of animal food. Mainly small mammals are taken, especially rodents, but snakes, frogs, and insects are sometimes included in the diet. Small birds are seldom taken.

Inhabiting semi-arid woodland and brushland, the Harris' Hawk nests in mesquite, yucca, and saguaro. A dark chocolate brown overall, it displays conspicuous chestnut shoulder patches, wing linings, and flanks. The long tail is white at the base and is tipped white. This species indulges in cooperative hunting, with several birds joining up to capture such prey as jack rabbits, which are too large and elusive for a single bird to hunt.

Swainson's Hawk has larger, narrow, more pointed
wings than other "buteos," but identification can
prove difficult, as its plumage is extremely variable,
with both dark, light, and intermediate phases.
Particularly a bird of the open plains, it can be seen in
soaring flight as it hunts its prey, mainly large insects.

6.
HUNTERS OF SNAKES, LIZARDS, AND REPTILES

In southern Europe, the Short-toed Eagle feeds almost entirely on snakes, for which reason it is sometimes called the Snake Eagle. In flight it shows almost completely white underparts, for which it might be confused with an Osprey.

The Long Crested Eagle is aptly named, with its long head feathers forming a most distinctive feature. Found in South Africa, south of the Sahara it occurs in lightly forested areas and grassland with scattered trees, where it feeds on rodents, reptiles, and insects.

Widely distributed, the Lizard Buzzard is locally common in East and Central Africa. It frequents open country, often cultivated areas, coconut plantations, woodland, the edges of forests, and wherever there are baobab trees. It hunts from a perch, mainly feeding on lizards, which gives the bird its name.

A Short-toed Eagle returns to its nest to feed its one surviving chick a recently caught snake. It is a widespread breeding bird in southern Europe; this eagle's nest site was photographed in Portugal.

SECRETARY BIRD *SAGITTARIUS SERPENTARIUS*

With its long legs and long neck, the Secretary Bird perhaps looks least like the accepted bird of prey. However, it comprises a single species of a single family within the order Falconiformes. Unlike all other hawks, though, this species hunts on foot, running after its prey, which are mainly snakes. These it chases in a zig-zag fashion, frequently flapping its wings. This is no doubt a means of distracting and disorienting victims before it stamps them to death, usually aiming at a point just behind the head. Larger snakes are often carried aloft in the bill and dropped onto hard ground.

Other reptiles are also taken, as well as small mammals and large insects, especially locusts. It is also fond of young birds and the eggs of other birds.

It is the crest of long plumes that suggest a bunch of quill pens stuck behind the ear of an old-time lawyer's clerk that has given rise to its vernacular name.

The Secretary bird ranges throughout Africa—south of the Sahara, except for the equatorial forested regions—inhabiting open plains and grass covered savanna, over which it wanders widely. It is not a gregarious species, usually working in pairs, but numbers are drawn together in the wake of brush fires when pickings become easy with injured and crippled creatures readily found.

Secretary birds are believed to mate for life. Unusually for birds of prey, the female is smaller than the male.

When settlers from Europe first saw this bird's crest of long plumes, which to them suggested a bunch of quill pens, it was little wonder they called it the Secretary Bird. Of all the Falconiformes this species is totally unlike any other member of the order and is placed in a family by itself.

7.
OWLS OF OPEN PLACES AND TEMPERATE AND TROPICAL FORESTS

The Burrowing Owl is quite easily observed when the nest site is known, as it perches conspicuously outside the nest burrow or on a nearby post during the daytime. When excited or nervous, it bobs up and down in an almost comical way.

A ground-nesting species, the Burrowing Owl is boldly spotted and barred, with noticeably long legs. Mainly found in middle America southward, it is a bird of open country, often favoring golf courses, airports and the like. Flight is low and undulating, often hovering.

BURROWING OWL *SPEOTYTO CUNICULARIA*

A bird of mainly open prairie-type country, the Burrowing Owl is found on the plains of western North America and Florida; it also occurs in suitable country throughout the West Indies as well as Central and South Americas, excluding the Amazon basin.

In general appearance, it is much like the European Little Owl (*Athene noctua*), being equally endearing, having a permanent quizzical expression, accentuated by frequent inclination of the head or rapid bobbing motions. Generally spotted above and heavily barred below, showing considerable white on the brows and throat, the eyes are bright yellow while the tail is short. The Burrowing Owl has long slender legs with bare toes, which are used to excavate its nesting burrow, hence the name.

The burrow can be quite a sizable construction, sometimes up to five feet long, generally sloping for the first few feet and then leveling out. As well as digging its own burrow, a Burrowing Owl will quite happily take over a prairie dog hole or even larger ones vacated by foxes. The nesting chamber may be lined with pieces of vegetation or feathers and other debris in which six to ten glossy white eggs are laid. Both parents take turns in the incubation process, which takes around twenty-eight days. The young take about three weeks to fledge. Interestingly, the young Burrowing Owls when disturbed in the nest produce a rattling hiss similar to the sound made by a rattlesnake—which can occur in the same region and use similar holes. This similar-sounding call may well be a deterrent to predatory mammals investigating such burrows.

After they are well grown, the young spend a great deal of time outside the burrow, but at any hint of danger rapidly disappear back below ground, to the safety of their nest burrow.

Active by day and also particularly at dusk and also after dark, Burrowing Owls prefer to hunt from some vantage point, such as an earth mound or nearby fence post if in the vicinity.

Large insects form a major part of the diet, especially grasshoppers. Amphibians, reptiles, and a variety of small mammals are also taken and, very occasionally, small birds.

The Burrowing Owl is aptly named, for it excavates its own hole. Here a bird sends the dirt flying as it scrapes away with its long legs. Sometimes, however, Burrowing Owls take over the existing holes of prairie dogs and on occasion will utilize a deserted fox or badger hole.

This action shot of a Burrowing Owl shows it about to pounce on a large insect. It frequently catches insects in midair and also takes amphibians, reptiles, and a variety of available small mammals.

Distributed sparsely throughout most of Africa south of the Sahara, Pel's Fishing Owl might be easily overlooked, not least due to its nocturnal activities. Nearly always found in pairs, these birds hunt separately, however, from a perch overhanging water or riverbank. From such a vantage point they seize fish from the surface. The toes are lined with sharp spicules to help secure slippery prey.

NORTHERN SAW-WHET OWL *AEGOLIUS ACADICUS*

A small owl, about seven inches long, the Northern Saw-whet Owl is about two-thirds the size of Tengmalm's Owl (or Boreal Owl), which it closely resembles, especially the juvenile. Reddish brown above and white below with reddish streaks, it has a reddish facial disk (lacking a dark border) and a dark bill. The head is large in relation to the body, the wings are rounded, and the tail is short.

The Saw-whet is a woodland bird inhabiting dense coniferous or mixed forests, wooded swamps and tamarack bogs. As might be expected, it is almost entirely nocturnal, and its behavior is not readily observed. It can be more easily viewed if its daytime roost, which might be a hole or some dense thicket, is discovered. Mobbing birds can often lead the watcher to find the hidden bird and when discovered, it can appear absurdly tame, permitting very close approach. At times it might even allow itself to be captured by hand. When it does fly, it exhibits an agility reminiscent of a woodcock as it dodges between the trees. In open settings it adopts a more bounding, undulating flight.

Saw-whets usually nest in holes in trees, frequently taking over the old nest hole of a woodpecker or flicker. A tap on the trunk of a tree with a likely-looking nest site will invariably bring the Saw-whet owl to peer out of its tree home, if a bird is in residence. No nest material is brought, with the wood chips created by the past users providing a suitable cradle for the five to six rounded, white, glossy eggs.

As is usual within the owl family, hatching takes place over the same period as eggs were laid; incubation begins with the laying of the first egg. The young hatch after about twenty-eight days, and an equal length of time elapses before the young are fledged and leave the nest.

The Saw-whet's food comprises mainly small mammals, such as mice, rats, shrews, and small squirrels, but it is a formidable predator and will take animals larger than itself on occasions. Some birds are also captured, possibly as they roost.

Quite a noisy bird—particularly in the breeding season—the Saw-whet's monotonous, oft-repeated, single whistling note proclaims its presence. However, its other less commonly heard call—a series of disyllabic notes that bear a close resemblance to the sound of a sharpening file being rasped back and forth on the teeth of a saw—gives this bird its name.

Confined to North America, birds generally move to the central and more southerly states during the winter months.

The Northern Saw-Whet Owl is so named because of its distinctive call: a series of disyllabic notes, which bear a close resemblance to the sound of a sharpening file being rasped back and forth on the teeth of a saw. This is most frequently heard in the early part of the year, peaking in intensity during the spring.

Large, forward-looking eyes are a characteristic of all owls and are well demonstrated in this photo of a Northern Saw-Whet Owl.

The Saw-Whet Owl is shown in its dramatic flight. Its usual home is the dense coniferous or mixed forests and wooded swamps across most of the United States.

BARN OWL *TYTO ALBA*

The Barn Owl is a cosmopolitan species, breeding in most parts of the world. In Britain it has been in decline, possibly due to lack of suitable nest sites, especially holes in old trees and barns. This photograph shows a bird in such a typical breeding location.

Perched in the opening of a barn nest site, two fully fledged young Barn Owls look out into a world that is full of danger for them. Many die by flying into overhead cables or are killed by motor vehicles, dazzled by car headlights, as they drift low over roads as they hunt at night.

The Barn Owl is one of the best-known and most widely distributed owls in the world and is found in North and South America, Europe, western Russia, Africa, southern Asia, and Australia, with several subspecies distributed throughout its range.

Barn owls are typified by their heart-shaped facial disk, white underparts, with the upperparts an orange buff speckled with dark gray and white. The nominate race, or White-breasted Barn Owl (*Tyto a. alba*), occurs in the British Isles, western France, Spain, Portugal, Italy, and countries bordering the Mediterranean, while the subspecies, *T. a. guttaia*, or Dark-breasted Barn Owl, overlaps with *T. a. alba* in eastern France, Belgium, and western Germany, where the two interbreed.

A very nocturnal species, it is more likely to be seen in the glare of car headlights as it sweeps low over a country lane during its hunting flights. This unfortunately sometimes ends in disaster when the bird, dazzled and disoriented, is hit and frequently killed by collision with the vehicle. However there are times when it hunts by day, usually during the breeding season when feeding its young, or during cold spells in the winter when prey is harder to come by. The flight is buoyant and virtually noiseless, comprised typically of a series of slow flaps alternating with glides and occasional bouts of hovering. Prey is caught by suddenly dropping or diving into it, grasping it with the long sharp talons, and usually swiftly crushing the life out of the unfortunate creature with its bill. The captured prey is often devoured on the spot, but might be carried to some more convenient location before being swallowed. When feeding young, the bird will take its prey to the nest site, sometimes still held in the talons.

The Barn Owl's main prey comprises small rodents, especially rats, voles, mice, and shrews, but occasionally young rabbits are taken. Small birds are also taken, and these are usually snatched from their roosting places. Bats, frogs, lizards, large insects, and even fish have featured among its less usual items of feed.

Like most owls, the Barn Owl generally swallows its prey whole, as long as it is not too large. Those parts of the prey that the owl cannot digest, such as bones, fur, feathers, or the chitinous parts of insects are later regurgitated in the form a pellet. Two pellets are normally produced every twenty-four hours. In the case of the Barn Owl, these are firm compressed, oval, and shiny black. These are "coughed" up at the nest site or roosting place, and many can be found at any such regularly used site.

By breaking down the pellets into fragments, it is possible to accurately determine what prey an individual owl is taking. All birds of prey, and owls particularly, are well known for this behavior, and the pellets produced by a particular species are normally quite distinct and recognizable, as in the case of this species.

Breeding starts early in the year; in Britain it is claimed egg laying has been recorded in virtually every month of the year. No nest as such is built, the eggs being laid on the floor of a crevice or hollow in an old tree or barn, a favorite nest site, as the name suggests.

The eggs are pure white and more pointed than those of other owls. As few as three may comprise a clutch, but between four and seven is usual. Incubation lasts from thirty-two to thirty-four days, with a fledging period of nine to twelve weeks. Quite often a pair will raise two broods in a year. As is usual with owls, incubation starts with the laying of the first egg, resulting in staggered (asynchronous hatching). This can mean great disparity in size and the development of the chicks, sometimes resulting in the last to hatch not surviving. In view of the Barn Owl's present status in Britain, this is not good news, for possibly due to the fact there are fewer old trees and traditional barns for it to nest in, the population of *T. alba* has been much reduced in recent years. This is causing concern for all those who care about Barn Owls. Long may their ghostly forms float across darkened fields or around overgrown churchyards. Long may we continue to hear the eerie screams and the peculiar grunts and hissing noises of young owlets that tells us Barn Owls are still with us, though there are many who may never see one in the normal course of their daily lives.

An adult Barn Owl adopts an aggressive pose to an unseen source of possible danger, perhaps a hunting farmyard cat. A young owlet protected by the parent is at the rear.

The White-faced Owl, with its black-bordered white face and large orange eyes, is possibly the most attractive looking of all the owls. It is a bird of the African savanna; this pair was photographed in Kalahari National Park, South Africa.

The smallest American owl, the Elf
Owl is a common bird of desert lowlands
and is also especially fond of oaks and
sycamores. Unfortunately ,it is in
decline in Texas and California. The
photograph shows a bird peering
from its nest hole.

The Barred Owl is a common bird of dense
coniferous or mixed woods of river bottoms and
swamps, but they also occur in upland woods.
Mostly found in the Eastern half of the United States,
this bird's range extends westward across Canada
and into Washington and Oregon. It has a distinctive
call, a rhythmic series of loud hoots, rendered as
"who cooks for you—who cooks for you all."
Though nocturnal, it frequently calls by day.

Widely distributed across the whole of the Northern Hemisphere and in the southern half of South America, the Short-eared Owl is probably more well known than some owls due to its diurnal behavior, hunting extensively during the daylight hours as well as at night. As the name indicates, it has short ear tufts, but these are rarely discernible.

SHORT-EARED OWL *ASIO FLAMINEUS*

The Short-eared Owl is widely distributed and breeds throughout much of the Northern Hemisphere, also in most of the southern half of South America. It is also found in such unlikely locations as Hawaii, Galapagos Island, and the West Indies, isolated from its major nesting range.

Over the main European, North American, and Asian parts of its range, there is only one subspecies, but there are another seven that have been described from other areas.

A medium-sized owl at around fifteen inches in length, the Short-eared Owl has rather longer wings than other similar-sized owls. These are broad and rounded with a dark patch at the carpal joint (or wrist), which shows on both the upper and under surfaces of the wing. The tail is longish and strongly barred. The body upperparts are boldly mottled with pale buff and dark brown. The underparts are generally pale and boldly streaked with brown: these are variable in both male and female birds.

The eyes are an intense yellow, the bird displaying an almost hypnotic stare. These are surrounded by dark-tipped feathers in pale facial disks. The so-called ears are barely discerned and at most times cannot be seen at all—they are, of course, feather adornments and are only raised at times when the bird becomes anxious or excited. Short-eared Owls inhabit open country, favoring moorland, marshes, dune islands, golf courses, airfields, and the like.

Although they are at their most active during the early morning or evening, they can be seen hunting throughout the daylight hours, quartering the ground with typical rolling flight, frequently gliding on wings slightly raised in a shallow V. When prey is spotted, the owl drops like a stone and invariably secures its victim with its powerful talons. Short-eared owls perch frequently on fence posts, poles, bushes, or any mound that gives an all-round view. At such times the body is held in a near horizontal position rather than the more upright stance of other owls. Prey is any small mammal, with voles a particular favorite. In plague years when voles are especially numerous, the numbers of Short-eared Owls increase dramatically. At these times they can be seen hunting in groups as they also do on occasions in the winter months. When voles are not so numerous they will turn to other prey, such as young rabbits, small birds, and large insects.

In northern Europe nesting may begin as early as March, with a nest created on the ground, normally a shallow scrape lined with grasses. Eggs are usually laid in late April or early May. These are white and round, with three to seven laid in normal years. This number can be as high as ten in years of peak rodent population.

Incubation lasts about a month, and the young generally fledge after another four weeks.

This portrait of a Short-eared Owl shows the facial disk feathers, which as for all owls are thought to operate as a means of concentrating sound into ears. These are slightly displaced on either side of the bird's head, providing a range-finding mechanism that allows it to more accurately pinpoint prey.

A Short-eared Owl is shown at its nest, a typical ground site in long grass. Some of the white, ball-shaped eggs can be seen. A full clutch may number as many as ten eggs. This usually occurs in years of peak rodent population, when there is an abundance of food to feed greater numbers of young.

LITTLE OWL *ATHENE NOCTUA*

A small, plump, compact bird with flat head and short tail, the Little Owl's grayish-brown plumage—spotted, mottled and barred with white—provides a distinctive combination of markings, enabling quick identification. Additionally, the facial disks are flattened above the yellow eyes, giving a fierce, frowning expression.

More diurnal than other owls, it can sometimes be seen perched on a telegraph pole or tree branch in broad daylight, when it is often mobbed by small birds. It also favors gates and posts, where it will sit in an upright position. When alarmed it bobs. Flight is undulating, recalling a woodpecker, though the Little Owl's rounded wings and general appearance proclaim its identity. It feeds mainly on insects, large beetles, and worms, but will take small birds, small mammals, and reptiles. Its call is a monotonous and rather plaintive "kiew." It has other less frequently used barking notes.

In Britain, the Little Owl favors agricultural land with plenty of trees and farm buildings, parkland, industrial wasteland, moorland edges, and coastal areas. In some parts of its extensive range, it is equally at home in semidesert regions and steppe land. Britain's population is estimate at around ten thousand pairs.

The Little Owl is not an indigenous British bird and was introduced during the nineteenth century, when first attempts in Yorkshire were unsuccessful. Extensive introductions near Oundle (Northamptonshire) around 1890 resulted in established breeding in the area, and it subsequently spread to nearby counties. By the early part of the twentieth century the Little Owl had extended its range to most of the Midlands and southern England. There have been some decreases in recent times, but it continues to spread slowly northwards; however, it is rarely noted in Scotland and Ireland.

An adult Little Owl tenderly passes a large moth to its young at the entrance of a typical tree hole nest site. Note that the adult bird's eyes are closed to avoid accidental injury by the young bird's beak—this, of course, is happening in total darkness and is illuminated for a brief second by the photographer's flash.

The Spotted Eagle-Owl is very variable in color, the commoner form being a gray color, as shown here. There is a rarer rufous or buff phase. One of the smaller eagle-owls, it feeds to a greater extent on insects, but does also take small rodents and birds. It occurs throughout the savanna regions of Africa and eastern Arabia.

The Flammulated Owl is mainly found down the eastern half of the United States and is common in oak and pine woodlands, especially ponderosa. In the north of their range birds are generally grayer, and in the south of their range they are noticeably redder.

TAWNY OWL *STRIX ALUCO*

The Tawny Owl is without doubt the commonest and most familiar owl over most of Europe, but its thoroughly nocturnal behavior means it is not always readily seen.

By day it roosts in a hollow tree or thick bush. If disturbed during the daytime, or perhaps seen on the wing at dusk, it appears as a moderately large bird with short, rounded wings and a large head. When viewed at close quarters, the rich, mottled brown plumage and conspicuous white patches on the wings can also be seen. Prey is mostly taken from the ground and includes mammals, especially field mice, field voles, and shrews. Some birds are also taken, principally starlings and sparrows, but other much larger species have been recorded. It has also been known to kill Barn Owls, possibly in competition for nest sites. Fish are not infrequent prey, with the occasional frog or newt. Quite often worms are brought to the nest. It ejects pellets of undigested material, as do other owls, but not at the nest site as the Barn Owl does.

There is a gray phase of this bird, but it is rare in Britain. The well-known hoot is a prolonged tri-syllabic "hoo-hoo-hoo" followed by a long, drawn-out, quivering "hooooooooo." This is regularly heard from mid-January to June and less frequently at other times. It calls occasionally before dusk and also has a distinctive "ker-wick" note uttered in flight.

The Tawny Owl is most at home in woodland, farms, and parks, but frequently is found in suburban areas where there are plenty of trees. It is rarely found in more open country.

In Britain, the estimated population of one hundred thousand pairs is generally distributed, though it is rare in northwest Scotland. It is unknown in the Hebrides, and also absent from the Orkneys and Shetlands and from Ireland.

A Tawny Owl peers from its daytime roost hole in a tree. Such a location might also serve as its nest site, while at other times an old crow's nest could be used. Occasionally the nest may be on the ground. A usual clutch comprises two to five white glossy eggs.

The Tawny Owl is one of the most common owls of Eurasia and northwest Africa. Its usual prey is small mammals, birds, frogs, earthworms, and insects. This bird just caught a House Sparrow.

SCREECH OWL *OTUS ASIO*

In North America there are two species of Screech Owl that were formerly considered to be separate forms of one species. These are the Eastern Screech Owl, found in the middle and eastern parts of the continent, and the Western Screech Owl, which is found mainly in western areas, as its name suggests.

Both are small owls with yellow eyes, have prominent ear tufts, and have a round-headed look, when the head is lowered. The Eastern Screech Owl has a pale bill, while the Western Screech Owl usually has a dark bill. The Eastern Screech Owl has underparts marked with bars and streaks, more strongly streaked on the upper breast. There is a red phase that predominates in the south of its range; a gray phase occurs in the north and in southernmost Texas. There is also a very pale gray form found in the northwestern part of its range. The Eastern Screech Owl inhabits wood lots, forest, swamps, orchards, parks, and suburban gardens, as does the Western Screech Owl, though the latter also occurs in deserts.

The Western Screech Owl is generally gray overall, but there is a brownish form found along the northwest costal zone. Both owls are nocturnal and are best located and identified by their respective calls, a series of whistles followed by longer trilling notes. They feed on insects, which are either seized by the feet when on the ground, or caught in midair with a loud snap of the bill. In winter, however, when there are no insects, small mammals, bats, birds, frogs, and invertebrates will be taken. Hole-nesting birds, they lay three to seven white eggs, which are incubated for about twenty-six days. The fledging period is around twenty-eight days, during which time the young are fed by both parents. Large prey is torn into small pieces in early stages. They continue to be fed by the adults for several weeks after they leave the nest.

This photograph shows a juvenile gray phase of the Eastern Screech Owl. Formerly classified with the Western Screech Owl as one species, the range separation is still not clearly defined.

A trio of young, gray-phase Eastern Screech Owls shows their disparity in ages due to the fact owls begin incubating when the first egg is laid, resulting in asynchronous hatching.

The Eastern Screech Owl is common throughout the eastern half of the United States and is found in a wide variety of habitats, including woodlots, forests, swamps, orchards, parks, and suburban gardens. It is heavily marked, with bars and streaks on the underparts, particularly the upper breast. A red phase of this bird predominates in the South, with a gray phase occurring in the north. In southernmost Texas, a very pale gray form exists. This photograph shows a bird leaving a nest box in a suburban garden.

The Spotted Owl favors thickly wooded canyons and humid forests, mainly along the West Coast of the United States. It is an uncommon, and decreasing, bird in America due to loss of habitat through logging activities; there is great concern for this bird's future.

The Scops Owl is found across most of Europe eastward through Russia, as well as India, Southeast Asia, China, Japan, and parts of the east Indies. Preferring areas of broad-leaved trees, open woodland, orchards, farmland, parks, ruins, villages, and small towns, this small owl's presence is usually determined by its monotonous, single bell-like note, uttered for long periods at night.

The Grass Owl is found in scattered locations from Cameroon to Kenya and in Angola, Zaire, Zambia, and Southern Africa. Looking somewhat like a large, heavy Barn Owl, its haunt is long grass, where it feeds on small mammals. A most unobtrusive bird, it is not easily detected.

8.
KINGS OF THE BIRD WORLD

GOLDEN EAGLE *AQUILA CHRYSAETOS*

The Golden Eagle is one of the world's successful birds of prey and is found throughout most of the Northern Hemisphere, frequenting mainly barren mountainous country. With its six-foot wing span, it is a large bird, with females even larger than the males, which is general among birds of prey (except the vultures). With its majestic, soaring flight, the Golden Eagle makes maximum use of air currents, rising on thermals to great heights, wings outstretched, the primaries separated like the fingers on a hand and slightly upturned at the tips. It spirals in wide circles as it seeks out its prey, which varies according to its availability, although Grouse, Ptarmigan, and mountain hares form a major part of its diet. Other bird species and mammal species are also taken, and in coastal areas seabirds feature prominently among its chosen prey. Like most eagles it also eats carrion and will feed on dead lambs. These it will take back to the nest to feed its hungry youngsters. This practice has, not surprisingly, brought into conflict with hill farmers, who automatically suspect that the Golden Eagle has actually killed the lamb. It is, of course, quite capable of taking a live lamb, but it rarely does so. In Scotland Golden Eagles have been killed by farmers putting out poison bait (which in any event is against the law) in the belief they are protecting their interests.

The adult Golden Eagle is a uniformly chocolate brown color, except for some golden feathering on the nape, which gives the bird its name. Young birds lack this golden color and show white patches in the wings, while the tail is white with a black band. These features often give rise to their misidentification as the White-tailed Sea Eagle.

The Golden Eagle's nest is a bulky structure of sticks, branches, heather stems ,and bracken, lined with

This portrait of a Golden Eagle shows the bird's powerful hooked beak, with which it tears its food into consumable portions. The golden brown feathers on the nape are obvious, a feature of its plumage that gives the bird its name.

An adult Golden Eagle comes down to drink or perhaps bathe at a mountain stream.

grass, ferns, and other fresh material. The nest site, or eyrie, is often reused over many years. It is often located on a cliff ledge or at times in a tree. A pair often use several nest sites in rotation, changing location each year. A clutch of two eggs is the norm, but occasionally it might be three and less frequently only one. These are dull white flecked and spotted with red brown and gray. There is normally a three-day interval between the laying of each egg. Incubation starts with the laying of the first egg, which means there is a staggered hatch producing two chicks differing slightly in size and strength. The larger, stronger chick invariably attacks the younger, weaker one, which often dies from such persecution and lack of food, most of which is taken by the stronger bird. The parents do nothing to redress the balance in this so called Cain and Abel conflict, which often results in only one chick finally fledging.

The young eaglet leaves the nest after about nine or ten weeks but stays with its parents for some considerable time afterward, learning the hunting skills so necessary for its survival during the first winter. In the following year the young eagle leaves its natal ground to find its own living space, though it will be at least five years before it becomes a mature breeding bird.

As with many birds of prey and, particularly in the case of such large, obvious birds as eagles, man's hand has been raised against them and many have been deliberately killed by shooting or poisoning. To a lesser extent egg collectors have contributed to their decline in numbers in some areas. The unlawful taking of eggs causes great concern to conservationists and bird protectionists. Every year in Britain, for example, the Royal Society for the Protection of Birds prosecutes egg collectors, whose special quarry is often the Golden Eagle.

In other parts of the world the Golden Eagle has been the subject of unwarranted attack. Several years ago in Texas, hunters in slow-flying aircraft regularly shot this bird. Hundreds of birds were killed, until this practice was finally illegalized.

As more and more people come to appreciate the grandeur of a soaring eagle and understand that they do not really threaten anyone's livelihood, it is hoped that these birds will become an even more common sight and will not be totally confined to those remote parts of the world where their shape, form, and beauty are not so easily observed.

This subadult Golden Eagle in flight displays some white in the wings; the white tail with the dark end band is very evident.

A Golden Eagle in low-level flight sweeps in along a hillside. The powerful talons are brought forward just before impact to snatch its prey from the ground.

In the safety of its cliff face eyrie, a male Golden Eagle tenderly offers one of its two well-feathered eaglets a small morsel of food. Very soon the young birds will be tearing up prey brought by the parent and feeding themselves.

The usual clutch size of the Golden Eagle is two eggs, occasionally three, but sometimes only one. These are flecked and spotted with red brows but at times they can be totally unmarked (except for some dirt), as those shown in this photograph.

An immature Steppe Eagle in flight in Oman, where it overwinters, as well as in the rest of Arabia and Africa. Some authorities regard this bird a race of Tawny Eagle (Aquila rapax), which is very similar.

The Bateleur, a large, handsome eagle, is a bird of the tree and bush savanna throughout Africa south of the Sahara and eastward into Arabia. Mammals ranging in size from small antelopes to mice constitute its main prey. It also takes birds and reptiles as large as monitor lizards.

111

A Tawny Eagle in a threat posture displays a menacing and intimidating appearance usually sufficient to deter any intruder from entering its territory.

TAWNY EAGLE *AQUILA RAPAX*

The Tawny Eagle, or Steppe Eagle, as it is also called, is probably the most numerous medium-sized eagle in the world and is to be found in a great diversity of habitats from semidesert, open, grassy plains, and well-wooded savannas to open cultivated country. This range extends throughout Romania, eastward through south Russia, south Siberia, and the Khirghiz Steppes to Mongolia and South Arabia, India, and almost the whole of Africa.

Throughout this huge area there is a considerable variety of plumage comprising a rather complex collection of closely related but sometimes quite isolated species or subspecies. The world's scientific opinion is still divided as to whether some of these birds are complete species or forms of a complete species. Within this group the general appearance of all Tawny Eagles is extremely variable, and there is no real identifiable pattern, with the body plumage almost wholly individual in character from almost white in color through brown to blackish. Some birds can be predominantly pale yellow or buff with extreme examples of ginger or marmalade.

The Tawny Eagle is very catholic in its taste for food and is a carrion eater, a scavenger, and also a killer of small birds and mammals. One of it major food procurement methods is to steal from other birds as small as Kestrels to those as large as a Martial Eagle. With some of the larger eagle species it is not always successful.

The northern races migrate over considerable distances, while those living in the tropics make more local, but regular movements. On migration birds travel in flocks and follow well-known routes into Africa mainly through Suez. In their winter quarters, Tawny Eagles are gregarious, and small flocks of twenty or more are not unusual.

As a prelude to nesting, Tawny Eagles soar to great heights, the male diving at the female, the flights interspersed with its barking call. Sometimes the two will grapple together, to whirl downward, talons interlocked.

Nests are built in trees from as low as ten feet to as high as one hundred feet above ground. They will also nest on the ground or on a crag.

One to three eggs are laid, the usual clutch is however, two, sometimes marked with blotches and spots of reddish brown, but sometimes unmarked. Incubation lasts about forty-five days, with a fledging period of up to fifty-five days. Nest losses of young and eggs are quite high in this species, especially with ground-nesting Tawny Eagles.

An immature Tawny Eagle swoops onto its prey hidden in the grass. With talons outstretched, it will crush the life out of its hapless victim.

Having just taken flight, this Tawny Eagle still shows its legs and powerful talons dangling, which it will bring up into the body to reduce drag when in full flight, as with aircraft.

A Verreaux's Eagle—clad in overall deep black plumage, which inspired its other common name, Black Eagle—gives a disdainful glare in the direction of the photographer. In flight this bird shows a conspicuous white patch on the rump with pale patches in the wing. The immature Verreaux's Eagle looks like a large, pale Tawny Eagle.

The largest eagle in Africa, the Martial Eagle weighs in at almost fourteen pounds. An impressive and fearsome-looking bird, it can bring down an impala, though it usually takes much smaller prey, especially Sandgrouse, Francolins, and other ground-dwelling birds.

A tree-loving species, the Spotted Eagle favors forests near inland lakes, rivers, and marshes. Here it is shown resting in migration while on passage through the Oman. Somewhat larger than the similar Lesser Spotted Eagle, it is distinguished by a paler crown and wing coverts; in flight it displays narrower wings held slightly forward with the sixth primary just discernible.

The African Hawk-Eagle is larger than the Augur Buzzard, but less numerous. Local and uncommon in its Ethiopian range, it frequents forested and savanna woodland, baobab country, and coastal forests, shunning inhabited areas. It is most likely to be seen in the national parks and coastal forests of Kenya and Tanzania.

A Buzzard-sized, long-tailed Eagle, the Booted Eagle occurs in dark and light forms, with the light phase being the most plentiful. It breeds in Spain, North Africa, the Balkans, Turkey, Greece, and as far east as Asia. A migratory species, birds from Europe winter in Africa, while Asian birds move to India.

The Wedge-tailed Eagle is widespread in Australia, which says much for its resilience, for it has been heavily persecuted. Many have been poisoned and shot over the years, even as recently as the early 1970s. It is now fully protected in most Australian states, which augurs well for its future.

Three downy Wedge-tailed Eagle chicks in the safety of their nest await the return of a parent with food. This is likely be a rabbit, a readily available food since they were introduced into Australia, rather than an endemic marsupial, which are now less numerous.

WEDGE-TAILED EAGLE *AQUILA AUDAX*

With a wing span of over eight feet, the Wedge-tailed Eagle is Australia's largest bird of prey. The overall plumage is sooty black, with tawny hackles on the nape; it has pale brown wing coverts and undertail coverts. The legs are feathered.

Immature birds are much paler than adults and gradually darken with age, the transition to maturity taking five or more years. The Wedge-tailed Eagle is aptly named for it is the long, tapering wedge-shaped tail, which is by far the best identifying feature, certainly when the bird is in flight. Other Australian birds of prey with which it may be confused are the immature White-bellied Sea Eagle, and possibly Black-breasted Buzzard, which both soar on long-fingered, upswept wings similar to those of the Wedge-tailed Eagle. However, the White-bellied Sea Eagle is confined to the coastal belt, whereas the Wedge-tailed Eagle is a bird of mainly open country throughout the whole of Australia, including desert regions. The Wedge-tailed Eagle spends much of the day on the wing often soaring to great heights, behaving much like a vulture in seeking out its prey. Also like vultures, they will gather in numbers at a carcass.

Though much of its behavior is vulturelike, it will catch some of its prey in fast, swooping flight, though its success rate is not high in this hunting mode. The breeding season is July to October. Usually two and rarely three eggs are laid in its tree-located nest twenty to thirty feet above ground, though at times this may be much lower in a bush or occasionally even on the ground. The female alone incubates the eggs for about four weeks. It takes another nine to ten weeks before the young are fully fledged, and it may be another three weeks after that before they can fly well.

The recent history of the Wedge-tailed Eagle has been bound up with the settlement of Australia and introduction of sheep and rabbits. This has undoubtedly altered its way of life and brought it into conflict with man. Probably no other eagle in the world has been so heavily persecuted, and for about one hundred years it was considered vermin in some parts of Australia, with a price on its head. It is reckoned 120,000 were killed during the 1950s; many were shot, but many more died from poisoning. Even up until the 1970s, Wedge-tailed Eagles were being killed. Though numbers have been greatly reduced in some areas, this resilient bird has survived.

9. FULL-FLIGHT ATTACKERS

PEREGRINE *FALCO PEREGRINUS*

The Peregrine is considered by many to be the ultimate flying machine and has long been admired for its prowess and aerial skills, even by those who are neither ornithologists nor falconers. Perhaps the most spectacular demonstration of its aerial prowess is its hunting procedure, when in direct flight it overhauls the intended victim (many species of birds are eaten), climbs above it, and at great speed, with wings half closed, hurtles downward in a slanting dive or "stoop" to fatally strike.

It has been suggested that its speed in this attacking dive is in excess of one hundred miles per hour, but in truth it is probably around sixty-five miles per hour; this speed is quite sufficient for the Peregrine to kill the victim outright. If not killed while in flight the bird prey is invariably killed by the impact of its fall to earth. It is the Peregrine's hind claw that does the damage, often ripping open the bird's back or completely removing its head. When the prey is retrieved it is usually partly plucked before being eaten. A pile of feathers is often an indication of a Peregrine in the neighborhood.

In coastal locations Peregrines can find plenty of suitable nest sites among the steep cliffs. In the breeding season there is also plenty of food to be found in such locations, among the many nesting seabirds.

The Peregrine in direct flight looks pigeonlike. This bird is immature and shows a more streaky breast than the barred look of an adult, but in all stages of their life the strong moustachial streak is very evident.

The Gyr Falcon is considered by some falconers to be superior to the Peregrine. Much larger than the Peregrine, it is also slower in direct flight. A bird of the arctic regions, it has both white and gray color forms.

KESTREL *FALCO TINNUNCULUS*

The hovering flight of the Kestrel identifies this bird immediately, for no other hawk has so perfected this mode of hunting. It hangs thirty feet or more above the ground on rapidly quivering wings, the tail frequently adjusted according to wind speed. The head is held down, scanning the ground for any movement that indicates the presence of a vole, mouse, or perhaps even smaller prey, such as a beetle or other insect. Having sighted its quarry, it dives headlong with almost closed wings to secure the creature in its talons. It is not always successful, but usually rises from the ground clutching its victim, which it devours at some quiet spot or regular plucking post.

In direct flight the long tail and pointed wings are distinctive. It often spends long periods perched just surveying the scene. The male has a slate gray head, rump, and tail, the tail having a black subterminal band and white tip. The back is rufous, spotted with black; the underparts buff with black streaks and spots. The bill and legs are yellow. The larger female is less colorful, displaying rufous brown with blackish barring above and a paler below with dark streaks. The tail is barred.

An Old World bird, the Kestrel is found throughout the whole of the Palearctic, Ethiopian, and Eastern geographic regions. In America, the American Kestrel (*Falco sparverius*) takes it place.

Present throughout the year in Britain, the Kestrel is that country's most numerous and widespread bird of prey, breeding in all areas except the Shetlands. The total population is probably in excess of one hundred thousand pairs.

The usual cry is a shrill "kee-kee-kee," and it can be very noisy at the nest site. It is generally silent at other times.

It favors woods, farmland, parks, moorland, and grass verges.

The Kestrel frequently uses the old nests of Crows or other large birds in which to raise its young, but often nests in a hollow tree, church tower, or other building, including ventilation openings and window ledges of factories or office buildings. It may also nest on the ground, particularly in the heather.

The four to five eggs are whitish, heavily marked with dark red-brown, laid in mid-April. It only has one brood.

Two young Kestrels stand at the edge of their tree hole nest site, ready to enter a world where their flying skills will determine whether or not they survive their first winter.

MERLIN *FALCO COLUMBARIUS*

A small, dark-looking falcon, the Merlin flies low and fast on narrow pointed wings, virtually hugging the contours of the land, only allowing the briefest of glimpses before it disappears over a rise in the ground or flips over a hedge or stone wall. Small birds form the major part of its diet, and these are usually secured in a short, twisting, turning chase, when the long yellow legs are thrust forward at the point of seizure and its agility and maneuverability are evident.

Birdwatchers lucky enough to spot a male will note that it is slate blue above, with a broad black terminal band on the tail, and the rufous underparts are heavily streaked. If the larger female is seen, perhaps only the distinctly barred brown and cream tail will register, for the dark brown back and streaky underparts are not so distinctive when the bird is in full flight.

On the nesting ground it utters a rapid, shrill, grating chatter, "kik, kik, kik-ik-ik," slightly lower-pitched in the female. In the breeding season the Merlin is a bird of upland areas, preferring open moorland. It also frequents sea cliffs and coastal dunes or, at times, open country and low-lying coastal areas.

The nest is a scrape in thick cover of heather or bracken, often on sloping ground or near the top of a hill or gully. The eggs, which usually number four to five, are thickly and evenly covered with reddish-brown stippling and are laid in early May, with only one brood.

The Merlin occurs in North America, and was formerly called the Pigeon Hawk, the

The long talons of the Merlin, shown here, enable this species to catch small birds more easily in its sudden bursts of rapid chasing flight. In the United State it was formerly called Pigeon Hawk.

plumage varies geographically from a very dark form of the Pacific Northwest to the pale form of Central Canada and the Great Plains. Generally an uncommon species, it is very local in the southern parts of its breeding range and rare in winter. In Britain the Merlin is present throughout the year. Not a common bird—and decreasing in number—it nests in Scotland, northern England, Wales, the southwest of England, and Ireland where suitable habitat occurs. The total population is probably now well under five hundred pairs.

As the name suggests, the Prairie Falcon inhabits dry open prairie country in the middle and eastern United States. It preys on small mammals and birds.

The Saker Falcon is a bird of open plains and desert-type habitats, breeding in middle Europe eastward into Asia. A bold and ferocious falcon attacking prey much larger than itself, it is greatly favored by falconers.

The Greater Kestrel, sometimes known as the White-eyed Kestrel, is found in East and Southern Africa from Somalia to the Cape. Favoring open country from desert to savanna, it feeds on small snakes, rodents, and ground-captured insects.

The Lesser Kestrel is a more gregarious and noisy bird than the slightly larger Kestrel (Falco tinnunculus). Its flight is also more agile. Gliding frequently, it rarely hovers, as the Kestrel often does. Its main diet is insects caught on the wing.

Slightly larger than the Peregrine, which it resembles, the russet crown and the pinkish unbarred underparts of the Lanner Falcon are good distinguishing features. Occurring throughout Africa, the Mediterranean, and the Middle East, it is found in most types of habitat. In South Africa it frequently nests in some of the larger cities, preying on the feral pigeon population.

Smallest and most numerous of the North American falcons, the American Kestrel is quickly identified by its russet back and tail and double black stripes on a white face. The bird nests in holes or cavities; this photograph shows the female returning to its nest with captured prey.

The American Kestrel was formerly called Sparrowhawk, but this is a term applied to the accipiters rather than falcons. In this picture, two fledglings peer from different holes of their tree site nest.

AMERICAN KESTREL *FALCO SPARVERIUS*

Formerly called Sparrowhawk, the American Kestrel is found in North and South America from near the tree line in Alaska and Canada south to Tierra del Fuego, though it is largely absent from heavily forested areas such as Amazonia. It also occurs in the West Indies, Juan Fernandez Islands, and in Chile.

Smallest and most common of the North American falcons, the male is quickly identified by its russet-colored back and tail and double black stripes on a white face. The crown is slate colored, often with a central rufous patch, while the wings are gray with scattered black streaks. These characteristics all combine to produce a most attractive bird of prey.

The American Kestrel is found in a great variety of habitats, from deserts to inner cities. Wherever it is found, the hunting procedure is the same: perching wherever possible on some elevated vantage point, it surveys the surrounding area for suitable prey. It can often be seen on telegraph wires, characteristically wagging its tail up and down. Its flight is buoyant, graceful, and rapid; when hunting, it habitually hovers like its Old World counterpart the Kestrel.

Its prey is procured either by plunging from a selected perch or often from hovering flight, when mainly insects are taken, especially grasshoppers in the summer months. In winter it is more likely to concentrate on small birds.

A hole-nesting species, the bird utilizes any natural hole, old Woodpeckers' hole, tree crevice, rocks, or buildings—and at times it will accept nest boxes. Three to seven eggs are laid, but a normal clutch is usually four to five. These are cream or pale pink, heavily marked with reddish brown. The female does most of the incubating, which takes twenty-nine to thirty days. The fledging period is around the same length, by which time the young birds can fly. The family stay together for some time afterward, forming a noisy, active group.

10. OWLS OF THE NORTHERN FORESTS AND TUNDRA

GREAT GRAY OWL *STRIX NEBULOSA*

At twenty-seven inches in length, the Great Gray Owl is one of the largest of all the owls. However, a great deal of its huge bulk is comprised of a high volume of feathers that provides insulation against the intense cold of the holarctic region, in which it is found.

The head is massive, as much as twenty inches in circumference which, with its large facial disk bordered with a dark ruff, creates an almost perfect circle, making it a most imposing creature. Additionally, there is facial barring formed by eight or nine concentric circles of brown on a white background. In the middle of these are a set of fierce yellow eyes, which further heighten the drama of this bird. However, the eyes look quite small for such a massive bird, say compared to those of the Tawny Owl. The eyes are also edged with black on the inside and in turn are bordered with two outward-facing streaks of white in the form of a comma. There is also a black bib that has white patches on either side. The rest of the plumage is a combination of whites, browns, and grays. The back of the head is evenly barred, the upperparts being mottled, barred, and streaked. The underparts are boldly streaked over fine barring.

There are two subspecies. One of these, which is found throughout Eurasia, looks paler, grayer, and more finely marked below than the other, which occurs in North America and is very coarsely barred on the belly. The two may be summarily described as white with gray-brown markings in the case of the Eurasian subspecies, and brown with white markings in the case of the North American subspecies.

Despite its size, it is surprisingly agile on the wing, and with slow, airy wing beats can maneuver easily between the trees of its forest home.

Found in northern coniferous forests it is, however, scarce and unevenly distributed. Though it is said to be Europe's rarest breeding owl there may well be more breeding birds than presently believed. It is largely resident in arctic Norway, Sweden, and Finland and has bred in Poland.

In invasion years (when voles are scarcest in northern Russia) Great Gray Owls move farther south over much of Scandinavia, Finland, and into the Baltic and occasionally reach eastern Germany. If sufficient food is available the following year they will sometimes stay to breed. In North America there is a much more defined migratory movement with birds moving south from the northern limits of their breeding range in winter, sometimes as far as Nebraska, Ohio, and New Jersey. Normally the Great Gray Owl takes over the old nests of other birds of prey, such as Goshawks, Ospreys, or Buzzards. It favors forests of pine and spruce within its European range, while in Canada poplar and larch forests are chosen.

Two to six white eggs, occasionally as many as nine, are laid in mid-April to mid-May. Incubation lasts about four weeks, with fledging slightly longer.

As with all owls, pellets are regurgitated, and study of these taken from several different sources has shown that voles comprise often in excess of three-quarters of the bird's total prey. However, some other mammals and some birds are known to be taken, mostly quite small species despite the bird's apparent ability to hunt down much larger creatures.

With its heavily ringed facial disks, the piercing yellow eyes of the Great Gray Owl look relatively small set in the face of this bird, which is North America's largest owl.

The Great Gray Owl inhabits the boreal forests and wooded bogs of North America and those of northern Scandinavia. It is also found eastward across Europe and through Russia, its breeding range almost encircling the Arctic.

With its large ear tufts, the Great Horned Owl could be mistaken for a Long-eared Owl, but this bird's greater bulk and size should distinguish it from the smaller, more slender, and less common bird in the United States.

Found throughout the whole of North America and South America, the Great Horned Owl is a large, bulky bird with long ear tufts. A common species, it occurs in a wide variety of habitats, from dense forest to open desert, even nesting within city limits. The photograph shows an adult and well-grown chick at a tree nest site, though it frequently nests in caves or on the ground.

GREAT HORNED OWL *BUBO VIRGINIANUS*

The second-largest North American owl, the Great Horned Owl occupies the same ecological niche as the Eagle Owl does in Eurasia. In fact the two species are closely related and apart from size differ in only relatively minor details of plumage color and pattern, suggesting perhaps they become isolated from each other in comparatively recent times.

The Great Horned Owl is found in most of North and South America, being only absent from the northernmost tundra regions of Alaska and Canada. Throughout this extensive range it occurs in a great variety of habitats, from boreal forest in the far north to the deciduous woodlands of middle America to rain forests of the Amazon basin. It is also found in desert regions and mountainous areas.

This bird is possibly one of the most familiar of owls to Americans, if not from actual observation but on account of its frequent film appearances, for often times this owl is included in nighttime scenes, particularly in horror movies, to provide atmosphere.

In any event its vocalizations widely proclaim its presence, particularly during the breeding season. At this time they make contact calls to each other through hooting. The male repeats a series of notes rendered "twit-twoot woo-oo." The first notes are brief and rapid with the latter more emphatic, the vowel sounds being extended. The female responds with a more raucous note, often creating lengthy nightlong duets.

For birdwatchers who go out of their way to view this bird, daytime roosts, when known, offer the best chance for protracted viewings of this most impressive owl. At times its often quite gentle look belies a most aggressive character, for in the breeding season, it will attack anyone that gets too close to the nest, especially when there are eggs or chicks.

Apart from its large size and large yellow eyes, this owl attracts attention with its prominent ear tufts. As in the case of some other owls and birds of prey, the Great Horned Owl varies in color and size, being larger where it occurs in higher latitudes and altitudes and smaller in lowland tropical forest and desert areas. Birds are also darker and richer in color in lowland forest areas than they are in the desert parts of its range. To further confuse watchers, there are two color phases, the orange-breasted and white-breasted. The frequency of these color phases varies from region to region, but in central Canada and Alaska, the white phase appears to be dominant.

The nest is usually in an old nest of a hawk or crow, or at times in a cavity in a tree or on a cliff ledge. The eggs, usually two or three, are white. Incubation is around thirty days, with both parents taking turns.

Hunting mostly at night or dusk, it preys on a wide variety of birds and small mammals, especially rabbits, rats, mice, grouse, ducks, and crows.

These two well-grown young Great Horned Owls could well be the survivors from perhaps a clutch of five, though two or three eggs are more usual. It takes twenty-eight days for the eggs to hatch— and at least as long again before the young are ready to leave the nest.

A Great Horned Owl grasps its prey before flying
to the nest site to feed its young. Though chiefly
nocturnal, it hunts by day, especially during the
nesting period, when there are hungry youngsters
to be fed around the clock.

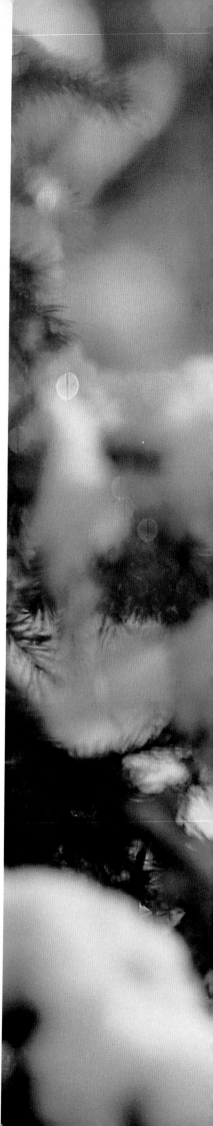

Tengmalm's Owl, or Boreal Owl, as it is better known in North America, is a bird of northern coniferous forests, especially spruce. The characteristic shape of its facial disk gives it a permanently surprised expression.

A Snowy Owl is shown in a snowy setting, typical of the type of habitat in which the species occurs. It breeds throughout the entire circumpolar tundra zone. This photograph depicts the female, which is white and heavily barred on the upperparts and underneath. The male is entirely white.

LONG-EARED OWL *ASIO OTUS*

The Long-eared Owl is the most nocturnal of the owls, seldom noted by day unless found roosting, when in an effort to remain undetected it presses itself against the trunk of a tree. In a relaxed posture it has a more squat, rounded appearance and in Britain might be mistaken for a Tawny Owl, but the ear tufts (they are not its true ears) and orange-yellow eyes are always distinctive. The upperparts are a beautifully marked mixture of brown and black with vermiculated grayish buff and dark brown; the breast is delicately streaked dark brown with wavy transverse barring, visible at close quarters. When seen in flight it looks grayer than the Short-eared Owl, its long wings also ruling out

the Tawny Owl, though the ear tufts then lie flat and cannot be seen.

Its prey includes small mammals, but can vary in some instances, being predominantly small birds, which are often taken as they roost, with a pair operating together, one flushing, the other catching.

During the breeding season it is found in mainly coniferous woodland and forestry plantations, but it also occurs in small belts or isolated stands of trees. Where common it is found in deciduous woodland. It also hunts over open country.

In North America it is uncommon, though sometimes comes together in small flocks during winter to roost during the day.

A resident species in Britain (also a winter visitor), it has a scattered distribution, being scarce or unknown in many areas, particularly the Midlands, southwest England, parts of northeast England, Wales, and northwest Scotland. It is fairly common in Ireland, where it replaces the Tawny Owl. Total British and Irish populations are probably not over ten thousand pairs.

One of the most nocturnal of all the owls, the Long-eared Owl rarely if ever hunts by day. Its food, predominantly voles, mice, and rats, can be captured in total darkness, the owls relying entirely on their acute hearing. This species also takes small birds, and a pair will hunt together, one flushing the quarry from a bush or tree, the other capturing it.

During the day, Long-eared Owls sleep in dark places invariably close up to the tree trunk and preferably in conifers. They will, however, roost in dense bushes, and in the winter several will often spend the night at such a location. Though mainly a sedentary species, northern populations tend to move south or west after the breeding season.

This portrait of a Long-eared Owl well demonstrates how this bird got its name. The tufts, however, are just feather adornments used in display and are not ears at all. The ears proper are at each side of the head, hidden by the head feathers.

The Eagle Owl, one of the most powerful and awesome of the world's owls, sits in regal splendour on a favourite rocky ledge. Despite an extensive breeding range, nowhere are they common and in Europe especially, they are increasingly rare and might even be considered endangered.

The Northern Hawk Owl shows a long-tailed,
falconlike profile and is indeed a fierce predatory
creature, favoring small mammals and other birds.
It inhabits northern forests and has distinctive barred
underparts and black-bordered facial disks.

PHOTO CREDITS